F*CK GROWTH

A Guide to Betterment in Today's World of Business

Jennifer Dodge and Jesse Nunley

Published by Thenticate, LLC. through Amazon.com

To our families, both in our homes and in our hearts. And to all those who believe in our vision. You all made this possible.

CONTENTS

Title Page

Copyright

Dedication

Foreword

Part 1   1

1. The Betterment Mindset   3

2. The Growth Mindset   14

3. Growth VS Betterment Mindset   26

4. Moving Forward with Betterment   40

Part 2   51

5. Betterment Operations   52

6. Betterment Products and Services   64

7. Betterment Leadership   76

8. Betterment Management   88

9. Betterment Teams   97

10. Betterment Culture   106

11. Betterment Marketing   118

12. Betterment Sales   132

13. Betterment Customer Experience   144

14. One's Own   151

Part 3   173

15. The Betterment Model   174

16. The Betterment Assessment   188

17. Betterment In Action   191

What's next?   203

Frequently Asked Questions   205

About the Authors   209

About Thenticate   211

A Farewell   215

FOREWORD

The Betterment Movement

Do you remember The Lorax by Dr. Suess? It's interesting that most of us have read that book when we were children, but most of the clients we talk to couldn't recite the message behind the book. The message of the book can be translated to business and is still more than relevant enough for today's world: our global economy can not sustainably support business as usual. In other words, we simply cannot keep doing the same thing over and over again hoping for a different or better result. Sounds a little like the definition of insanity doesn't it? We cannot sustain life or business in the long term if we keep supporting business as usual.

It's crazy that this seemingly simple yet very important message from our childhood hasn't stuck with us as a society when we reach our adult lives. It seems to have been programmed out of us and replaced instead with the promise and pursuit of more, more, more.

This book is a calling to get back to basics and doing the right things in business. It is a calling to create a better way of conducting business. A way that will create a movement of more conscious capitalism before the idea that the bottom line in our business is the only growth indicators that truly matters spreads its roots even deeper into future generations of entrepreneurs and young business owners.

This idea of what business success is supposed to look like is something we all have experienced at some point or another in our careers. More importantly, this idea has been ingrained in our minds by employers or instructors. We are trained and wired to focus on what appears on the bottom line above all else. We are encouraged to put the joy that being in business can actually bring to us and the world on the back burner because of this race to, well, no one really knows where. We are trained to make decisions driven by numbers such as units sold, overall revenue, cost of resources such as staff members and expected growth rate. Most of us have been taught that exclusive, top-down leadership is the most efficient way to drive company profits.

We wrote this book to shake up that isolated growth mindset by suggesting a more holistic way of looking at business. We are here to explore what real overall success can look like when you think differently and more broadly, and begin to see the impact on your business financially, personally and globally. And, the irony of it all is that those numbers we have been so solely focused on will actually positively change, sometimes dramatically, when there is a sincere shift in mindset to a better model.

A solid focus on the numbers like sales revenue, overall expenses, and how it impacts that bottom line growth is very important and our approach would not suggest otherwise. That is, after all, how the bills get paid and frankly how we pay ourselves, our internal resources and our vendors. Bottom line growth is an essential component of a healthy business. It takes financial wellness to expand and continue to create new products, new opportunities and new expectations for the future. We do not oppose this basic principle of business.

However the focus solely on growth for the sake of the numbers does not really tell the story of the business at all, and can actually be detrimental in the long run to broad, sustainable growth. In fact, an isolated focus on one aspect of growth can actually lead to an unhealthy overall business because the environment within the business is also impacted. And, not usually impacted in a positive way. Think about this: what is the true impact on business when customer loyalty is low? What dictates the actions of sales when it comes to time spent on customer acquisition? And, what about the cost of staff turnover when it feels like your business is a revolving door for employees? What is the financial impact on your business when your local community is divided in some way against your company's actions or products?

This happens because only one aspect of the business is being considered and all decisions are being made based on that narrowly defined element of success. When all aspects of a business are not considered, decisions are made in a vacuum, having a potentially devastating impact on other areas of the business. This results in a truly unhealthy and unsustainable business.

In this book, we will explore what it means to take a step back and look at the whole business, all the whys and the what-fors. What we are talking about are aspects that come from questions such as,

Why did you decide to go into the business that you are in today?

Why did you choose the team members you have chosen to help you reach your defined success?

What drives you to go to work each day?

What keeps you up at night?

What drives your passion?

Why do you work the hours you've chosen to work?

And, beyond those personally motivating questions, we need to be asking,

Why is our cost per customer high or low?

What are our customers' favorite things about our business?

What drives our staff to provide input and be accountable?

This is just a small sampling of the many aspects that can impact a holistic view of your business and each one is important to the overall sustainability of your business.

It is about a new mindset beyond the traditional growth mindset. It is about creating a better business by going back to what is truly important and what truly motivates you, your team and your customers. We will explore the bigger picture and also go beyond the traditional "bigger picture" to involve our lives, our families, our teams, and our communities.

As you read through the pages of this book, you will discover ways to uncover your true purpose in yourself as well as the true purpose within your business. This uncovering of that reason or purpose is one of the key foundations of creating a better business. This results in a more successful business, whether it be in sales growth, team growth, better efficiencies or community participation. And all of these things impact the bottom line. This occurs because of the drive, commitment and clarity it brings in each decision making process.

When you get back to all of those reasons you or those who founded your company started a business or got into the industry you are in today, you remember the passions, the commitments and the connections to that "why." Diving deeper into your business reveals the story of culture, connection and communication that is vital to whether or not you enjoy what you do. Not to mention, the energy you put forth to your team, family and customers will have an equally large impact on the future of your business.

And, you may find yourself creating new products, adding to your team, and even getting involved in your community in new ways that are meaningful and truly make sense for your bottom line. You may even find your personal relationships taking on a whole new meaning. This is because there is a mindfulness and purpose about your decision making process. Because you have taken the time to really dive into the various aspects of your business, you are able to see the overall health of that business with clarity and definition. In many ways, it makes it easier to make decisions such as adding team members or even creating new offerings based on your strategic planning.

As you go through this book, you'll discover ways to create that betterment in your business through taking a look at your operations, your sales and marketing process, your product development and even your community involvement.

It's also an incredible thing to watch you take this journey and see that betterment results in true, sustainable and transparent growth in your business and in your own life.

This is your pursuit of truth. This is the pursuit of integrity in business.

PART 1

*The Growth Mindset Versus
the Betterment Mindset*

1. THE BETTERMENT MINDSET

W hy does the idea of creating a mindset focused on business betterment really make a difference?

Think about and compare these words:

Better: more exceptional, effective, efficient or higher quality.

Growth: to develop by increasing in size or changing properties.

Can you see how focusing on the latter may lead to dissonance and conflict in a business? It is primarily focused on the size. If every business decision came from the filter of increasing size and changing for the sake of staying size-relevant there would hardly ever be a conversion or strategy for quality. This is because of the lack of acknowledgement of the core aspects of a business that will ultimately impact it, such as resources and customer impact. By the way, this isn't hypothetical. This is happening every day in business.

If you stop and think about the business practices of businesses you know, or the one you are in, who currently has the approach of the growth mindset, this concept becomes even more clear. Do you know a business that makes decisions because, "more revenue is a necessity based on a review of the profit and loss statements."? Let's say they want to grow by 20 percent. They then back into that number by adding new products based on this need for revenue growth, increase prices to help meet that goal and maybe even cut resources expenses or quality (cost of goods) to increase their bottom line. It is all about that numbers and more, more, more.

What is missing in this approach is the deep thoughtfulness of how to achieve this 20% increase in revenue. A different approach to reaching the revenue number would be to consider such aspects as product development and sales and marketing functions. The product development team would be engaged for input on how current products and services are meeting the needs of customers and what else could be offered to meet those needs better. The sales and marketing teams could then provide feedback based on what they are hearing directly from customers based on needs, quality and pricing. Along with input comes the questions around messaging and relationships built with customers, not to mention internally. By creating these conversations, solid strategies can be planned and executed that make more sense to reaching that number.

We want to start this chapter with an easy analogy to what we mean when we speak of betterment in business; personal health and development. With personal health and development we intuitively know that the key to success lies within the building blocks of fitness, life-style, and diet on a solid foundation based on commitment to self improvement. Success to self betterment lies in creating collaboration between all of those building blocks. Business betterment can follow that same process of thinking and honestly thrives in it. you simply need to know what the building blocks of business are and then the rules to success in each block. That is that this book offers.

We hear and read a lot in psychology and biology about ideas that having a full and satisfying life comes with the activities associated with self care and emotional intelligence. That idea also includes such activities as doing things with intent and purpose and creating more balance in life. These components combined are often considered the key to creating success and fulfillment. We intuitively know that we have to work on creating a better version of ourselves in order to navigate a world, body and life that is constantly evolving. However, in all of these readings, we rarely hear that "more" and "bigger is better." The ideas of being more mindful and purposeful are also the foundation of the business betterment model. the rules found in this book really are self-care and emotional intelligence strategies for your business.

Let's assume we are going to work on a personal vision board for a minute. We may find ourselves filling boards with pictures of vacations or homes on the beach or in the countryside. Now, stop and think about why we choose those items. Is it because bigger is better or is it because, for you, they represent ideas such as serenity, family, or the relaxation and freedom that you feel you would achieve if you had those things in your life? In other words, contentment isn't always tied to simply having those big "things." Having said that, we don't lose sight of the fact that many things that bring those feelings of contentment do take money.

When it comes to finding purpose and meaning, we rightfully turn to what feeds our internal selves. What does this mean? It means we engage in activities that give us those feelings of contentment and success while feeding our passions. Now, that passion is different for everyone, and it could mean anything from a passion for competition, helping people through business solutions or volunteering for local organizations and even all of the above. We nurture those ideas and visions because we know that doing activities that bring contentment leave us with feelings of happiness and success. We find our passions and our purpose, and we grow those activities because that's what drives us. That's the internal joy we want to experience on a daily basis. And when we use this same approach in our business activities it brings a balance that will have a profound impact on the business as well as in our personal lives.

So, taking all of these ideas to business, what if we went back to the actual "why" of why we're doing what we do?

What if we stopped to think about what's important beyond the day-to-day functions of a business? This is one of the most important first steps to business betterment.

What if, while we're looking at those spreadsheets and those staff issues, because we still need to do that, we dig deeper and look at the "why" behind all of those activities. Why are the numbers 'good' or why are they 'bad' according to your current decision making criteria and definitions. And, we don't mean just in the negatives or the positives in the numbers. Dig deeper. It's time to truly find or reconnect with the "why" of your business. And that means finding the "why" in every area of the business from culture to customers to resources including product development, sales and marketing. This is the first task we are asking of you.

This is where the idea of business betterment starts to come in to play as an approach to creating those same building blocks on a solid foundation that will lead to overall sustainable growth.

Not only are we bombarded with the concept of how important personal betterment is to the quality of life, it is also very apparent that there is a direct correlation between the way we act towards employees, customers, distribution, and towards our own selves and the overall impact on the success of a business. The same authenticity and attitude we bring to ourselves is the same attitude we bring to our business.

Think about how creating a life of fulfillment manifests itself through the attraction of people more in line with your own thinking and even in your own motivation and accomplishments. In fact, as you create that life, your loved ones and other people around you will take notice and will be attracted to that new energy you've created. Imagine that same attraction and energy in your business from the quality of employees you hire and the customers you attract, not to mention the strengthening of each of those relationships.

It's a magnet. People want to be around other people that invoke a positive experience. And so begins the foundation of trust.

What we are really talking about when it comes to business relationships is similar to the law of attraction. Whenever we bring this up in business we sense a hesitation to something that seems "far out" and ethereal. The law of attraction isn't a "far out" concept, it is concrete. How? While most people think about "positivity" as a thought process, and that positive things that they want will then magically come their way, that is not what we are necessarily talking about. We are talking about taking this concept and applying action to put it into practice. Instead of trying to be positive and hoping things come our way, we actively use positivity to fuel our actions and engagements. We do so strategically and with purpose. In this way, positivity is a tool and business resource that we can leverage. It is anything but "far out".

Now back to your business. We keep saying this, but it really is the same concept. People, which includes employees, vendors, customers, and anyone else coming into contact with your business are attracted to honesty, integrity, positive solutions and solid values. They remain loyal to businesses who share their values and have their best interests in mind. The return is positive impact on your bottom line.

The actions that you take are seen and absorbed by everyone who is involved in your organization. The higher up you are, the louder your actions speak. The louder your actions speak, the more impact they have in an organization. So, if someone in upper management makes a decision based on fear and scarcity like cutting resources or quality in a seemingly arbitrary way that leads to unethical or unsustainable decision making, what do you think the trickle down effect will be? To employees? To customers? To vendors?

The answer is somewhere between marginally negative to absolutely catastrophic. It is dependent on the gravity of the decision, the intent and honestly how "lucky" the company gets for how long. But either way, when looked at seriously, no one wants to be on this spectrum in business.

This is what we mean by positively attracting positivity. If decisions are viewed as less than transparent or honest, or if there is a disconnect or discontent among the employees, that positive energy does not exist and can actually perpetuate feelings of distrust and fear among team members and even customers. Actions create a re-action. And actions always stem from the thought process and belief systems within an organization. This is the root cause of success, and of failure in a business. And those processes and systems are what we are here to address.

In order to create a better business that sees sustainable growth in the long term, it is imperative to do things better and with a focused intent: better care of your employees, better care and solutions for your customers and better community citizenship. It also means true authenticity and true transparency. Once you fully believe in this betterment mindset and concept and embrace it, you will be amazed at the types of clients, customers and employees you attract and the impact on your success.

Having only a growth mindset may actually hinder sustainable growth as it doesn't prompt you to dig deeper into what actually turns the wheels of your business. It can prompt a narrowly-focused approach to decision making. What are the spokes connected to at the core of your business? What really drives your business? It's not the spreadsheet. Once you really dig deep and fully understand all aspects and people in your organization, that's when you can begin to have a business betterment mindset, and are successfully redefining growth.

If you work on becoming a better business, whether it is better operations, better staffing, better products, better services, better *everything* then your business will, without reservation, grow. Through a betterment mindset, you dive in looking for the successes and challenges of your business that you have defined by answering the tough questions instead of constantly trying to treat the symptoms when you do find those challenges. When many businesses see a problem, they tend to only look at the surface. For example, if a business finds that sales revenues are decreasing, they may choose to raise prices, create new products based on revenue need, cut resources such as staff, or reduce the quality of the product to reduce the negative impact to the bottom line. But this is really only treating the symptom of a shrinking revenue line. Utilizing the business betterment model, a business would dig deeper and ask the tough questions: is the product actually meeting the needs of the customer? Is it delivered in a manner in which the customer prefers? What about your staff? Are they standing behind the product? Do they understand how the product benefits the customers? Do they deliver the highest level of customer service? While these are just a few of the questions a business will need to ask, using this basic example we can represent the depth needed to begin to fully understand the workings of a business.

Ultimately, a betterment mindset leaves you truly understanding what everyone involved wants from the business, what they want for themselves and what they want for the customers, not to mention what the customer expectations are in actuality. There's a much bigger and better buy-in from the entire organization. When a business engages with their customers, staff, vendors and even the community, everyone has a stake in the game. Going even further, by communicating, engaging and asking for input, transparency is created that leads to a sincere trust. This trust allows for an authentic and safe input by customers and team members creating an opportunity for change that is based on the actual reality of needs and wants. This can be very powerful in the long run as decisions become more about what is best for the customer based on the expressed and practiced values which gets to the core of the business and its mission.

Betterment as an idea takes a refinement of what we except as ideals in our culture as well. In our world, right
now, it seems as though the emphasis is on the idea of
success or failure. This black-and-white attitude has
been around for generations, and we think it is time to
redefine those ideas. We hear in personal development a
lot about gratitude and kindness. This is something most
of our parents tried their best to teach us. We have noticed that when these concepts of compassion or empathy within an organization aren't present, there is usually a lower level of success, in every sense of the word.
The challenges that we are presented with in these organizations are employees that "just won't listen" and customers that "just don't get it" or "don't appreciate our
products/services". Oh, they might have a stellar sales
record. But look deeper. Look at the turnover rate of employees or the cost of the medical premiums not to mention high turnover of customers resulting in a higher cost
of customer acquisition. Oftentimes, in these organizations, those higher costs are due to that lack of understanding, compassion and empathy and they will result
in lower bottom lines in the long term, regardless of
what the quarterly reports are saying.

The betterment mindset doesn't happen overnight. It
takes some organizational soul-searching, some research
and some heart-to-heart conversations with your business partners, with your family, with your staff, and with
your clients. It will definitely take some work and a commitment to getting back to doing what's right and recognizing the true impact on your business beyond the rev-

enue or savings and compromise to increase that bottom line. As you go through the process of digging deeper into the business, you will begin to see how huge the impact could be to your professional and personal life.

Imagine what your organization could be capable of achieving. Imagine what you yourself could be capable of achieving and changing when it comes to creating fulfillment for your business. Not to mention for your customers and your own life when you commit to the process of business betterment and dive deep into your business to discover all of the "why's." And once you discover and answered all the questions, you create the action necessary to put solid decisions into place to create that success you have been looking for. That's incredible and sustainable. In other words, that's better.

2. THE GROWTH MINDSET

T he Growth Mindset as we define it in this book is based on the narrowly-focused emphasis on very limited factors. Those factors are believed to not only dictate growth, but to also create an environment that bases opportunity for growth solely on the numbers. The growth mindset does not consider other aspects of a business such as personal growth, engagement, communication, true leadership and trust as valid foundations and indicators of sustainable growth.

This mindset cannot continue as a rule in our world anymore. And here's why. It is simply impossible to anticipate, plan or work towards success without understanding the depth of what it will take to achieve our defined success. In order to achieve strategic goals in a business, it is absolutely vital to consider all aspects of a business from the numbers in that spreadsheet to the employees and their commitment to leadership to sales and marketing and most importantly, to the customers and how all of this ties to our values and missions. If we do not have a full understanding of what the business is really made of, then we will never be able to create a commitment to the common goals and drive the business forward.

The fall of the growth mindset really comes down to one concept: sustainability. We could break that down further into subsections and will do so within the pages of this book, but really it comes down to the ability to create sustainability or at least the inability to sustain solid growth based on well-rounded decision making. That well-rounded decision making centers around understanding all aspects of the business.

If you stop and think for just a moment about what a pure, simple and traditional growth mindset actually means to an organization, it's pretty astounding. It means that decisions regarding resources, customers, culture and even the mission are made in a vacuum. It is like putting together a puzzle without all of the pieces. You never know what the full picture is.

We have found ourselves completely and totally focused on the numbers as they pertain to sales, return on investment and expense line items. Most of us have experienced this growth mindset way of doing business at some point in our business careers. It has been nothing but the numbers that have dictated our decisions. We use the numbers to justify business actions to a board of directors, or our management team, or to ourselves, or our business partners, or even maybe our spouses. We all know the lingo: growth strategies, market penetration, diversification and acquisition among the long list of others that have historically pertained to numbers-only focus when it comes to growth. But what does all of this really mean to you and to your business. When we have traditionally said "grow" your business, these are the things that naturally come to mind. We think spreadsheets and bottom line figures and cost of goods and overhead and staff. We think management issues, staff issues, operational issues.

With a growth mindset, it is generally left to just a couple of top tier executives, the board of directors/investors or the owner of the business to decide what defines growth and success. Yes, at the end of the day, every organization must have those decision makers or someone that must take responsibility to move the business forward. But, what if those same people approached the business from a betterment mindset instead of a growth mindset with the narrow view of the spreadsheets and management reports? What if the betterment of the overall business and organization were contemplated, right down to what community involvement was important for bettering the business? Along with those spreadsheets, great things can happen with a broader mindset.

For a small business owner, when we ask, "why do you want to grow?" The answer is usually, "Because I am not making enough money." Makes sense, right? It's pretty straight forward. However, this comes from a place of scarcity and has nothing to do with product quality or customer satisfaction. Therefore any decisions made and actions taken come from that place of scarcity, i.e. the need for money, are inherently impulsive preventing deeper planning and a decision making process that leads to sustainable returns on investments made. The growth mindset does not give itself a chance for success.

In a larger business with a larger infrastructure, the decision-making within an organization defines how growth is actually possible and how it happens. Let's think about how that growth is determined...usually in a room with spreadsheets and by a smaller group of people generally in upper management positions. It usually doesn't initially involve thinking about the customers and whether their needs are actually being met or not. It is usually more focused on profit and loss, overhead and resources, growth and retraction instead of a full picture that involves all aspects of the business. It usually does not engage those team members directly interacting with customers or assembling products and service packages. We are not talking about simply that view from 30,000 feet that we discuss when creating strategic plans, or the desire to take a look at that sweeping view from above in this context. The answers regarding customer satisfaction and sales are usually left to the sales team or even a product manager. The sales team is then, independently, tasked with determining what will make the customer buy their organization's products and services. Simply put, again, a traditional growth mindset doesn't start with the customers. It starts with numbers. The marketing department often is an afterthought and is expected to back into the brand messaging based on a one-sided conversation.

When we stop to think about it, we can instantly hear the executives we've worked with in the past rebuke this now, "That's not true! We always think about our customers, staff and resources." And while that is likely true to an extent, but in true transparency, if we asked, "How were those decisions made?" The answer would almost never be, "With input from staff, customers and...." Instead, it would be a more politically savvy way of saying, "We decided what was best for them based on the numbers we received, and what we believe our customers need in order for us all to be successful." That isn't enough because, again, it does not take multiple important data points into consideration, such as direct input from the customers regarding why they use products and services, or what they like best about them or about us. It doesn't take into consideration what challenges they find in working with us, with our team or with our business overall. Nor, does this cover such aspects as employee loyalty, growth and contentment, or perceived culture as it relates to business values.

That's the growth mindset--what will initiate the sale and meet expectations based on the numbers put forth, and what will the numbers indicate to meet even more numbers. The numbers on that spreadsheet say things like: the cost per customer, the cost per product, the cost for marketing, total products and services sold, total revenue and of course the bottom line.

All of this information is very important, of course. This is the basic information we need to make basic decisions about the basic success of our business. We don't want to underestimate this information in the overall planning process.

But does it really give us what we need to truly understand where our business really stands? Does it really tell us the whole picture of business health? The health of a business goes far beyond just an analysis of the numbers based on whether they are in the red or black. It dives into all of those aspects that determine the real and authentic "why" the numbers are positive or negative.

Here is the potential downfall of the traditional growth mindset: it doesn't really give us a true understanding of the state of our business. How could a narrowly-defined mindset give us a full picture on the health of our business, not to mention the potential of long-term success.

Think of the stereotypical picture of "corporate america." This picture is often conveyed as cutthroat, cruel and uncaring about employees and customers. It's often conveyed as having top management that is only interested in themselves and their annual bonuses. We hear stories of employees downgraded to nothing more than an employee number, afraid of losing their jobs or feeling insignificant. How can we expect these people to be committed to the outcome of our goals? We hear of customer backlash and feeling betrayed or disconnected from products or services. How can we expect to meet sales goals if we aren't even aware of what is driving this disconnect and discontent? And, we hear of a complete dissonance between stated values and customer service. How can we expect to move forward if our services are not aligned with our mission and values?

Hey, bonuses are great aren't they? Wouldn't we all love to either receive one, or better yet, if we are the owner of the business, wouldn't we love to give ourselves and our employees one? Wouldn't it be great if these incentives were built into our plans based on a broader mindset that made sense?

These ideas are not limited to large corporations, by the way. We most often hear about them in the media with the more well-known brands. These ideas and perceptions exist all the way through many small businesses. But it can all change.

More importantly, let's get to the root cause of this growth mindset thinking. How could it have been possible for this stereotype to foster and grow? That root cause is exactly the growth mindset and it is exactly why, in many cases, we will begin to see the fall of the traditional growth mindset. The root cause is our desire for more and bigger when it comes to growth with very little regard for the importance of a foundation and building blocks that create a sustainable growth. It's a fight or flight, tunnel vision approach to business.

Basically put, it is a complete and total disconnect, from the top to the middle, to the sales and marketing team, and all the way to the end-user, the customer. In many cases, a job is a job is a job and the employees involved may not even understand what (or even care, quite frankly) why they are doing what they are doing? The job becomes a means to an end with no true commitment to the product, or worse, to the customer. And, the impact of these actions in practice is a deterioration in the growth of a business.

The sales team is tasked with making the sale. The marketing team is tasked with paving the way and creating the "message" whatever that might be given any day of the week along with the support materials with all of the claims that the sales team has determined will make those sales. And, often the marketing team is held responsible for the sales numbers without a full picture of the market reality. They are brought in to "help" either after the fact or without a full scope of information on all aspects of the business that are impacting sales.

What is missing here is the "we're all in this together" mentality. It is the sales team saying to the marketing team, "hey, our customers are saying that they really love the fact that our client center is open 24/7" and the marketing team incorporating that into the materials. It is taking that message to the client center and saying, "nice job! It's because of your hard work that we increased our sales. What's your secret?" It is the management team asking the production team what is the most efficient way to build a widget is or how to best deliver a service. And it is the production team asking the front line builders for their opinions on efficiencies and operations. And, it is asking the customers what keeps them up at night, what challenges they face and how you can help. It is the volunteer time spent down at the local charity of choice that fits in with the mission statement of the organization or was chosen by an employee based on a personal experience. And this is just scratching the surface. All of these activities build the brand credibility and value of the business.

So what happens when you and your business continue to stay on the path of the growth mindset? What happens when you only focus on those spreadsheets and nothing more?

There cannot help but be a fall out and deterioration of mind, body, growth and sustainability. The level of frustration from not understanding fully the business or the consequences of a growth-only mindset begins to build more and more and more over time. More importantly, it is one of the main reasons for the stress and tension you feel right now. Every day.

Think about it this way. You have a body builder who does his work religiously to build his muscle mass. He gets bigger and bigger, body wise, but doesn't focus on anything else. Then you have an individual who, through steadiness and focus, exercising regularly but also focuses on a healthy diet and regular check ups with his health care team along with getting stronger.

As the years go on, the body builder is unable to sustain the kind of growth he is used to if he continues to focus on only one aspect of overall growth and wellness. His or her large muscles use more energy, but aren't getting what they need. The body builder develops deficiencies and spends his latter years in pain and frustration, unless he makes a change.

The more balanced individual, that put energy in to all aspects of health, may not be able to lift as much in his prime, but can freely move and experience life the way he or she wants to up until the end of their life.

When you focus on growth for the sake of growth, there really is no way to continuously sustain or survive or experience the optimum experience we as business owners or executives can experience.

In fact there is almost an isolation of sorts that is occuring. We talked about the need for community. Creating community for your business as well as for life balance is what works to create that sustainability. The community in this example are all of the aspects of the individual working on his or her health: what and who they rely on for fitness, diet and support.

If a business only focuses on the bottom line, paying no attention to their community of employees, customers and those relationships along with their community of civic leaders and organizations, they cut themselves off from sustainability and broader growth through a business betterment mindset. There is a lack of broader thought which contributes to the overall health of the business.

I'm sure we all can name a few businesses that didn't survive, and when we look at any of them deeper we can see that their downfall was a result of some or many forms of a growth-only mentality. What we see in those businesses who have failed as a result of this growth-only minded mentality, are decreases in employee retention due to unhappiness in the workplace or even wages that increase. We also see a deterioration in the quality of product or services directly related to a narrow focus on expenses as they related to the cost of services products and the cost of delivering them, i.e. staff and customer service. And, overall a stagnation of growth, as opposed to a sustainable growth becomes the inevitable outcome. It's not if, but when this will occur.

As one final nail in the coffin of the growth mindset, let us take a look at India. At a point in the past, India ceased all importing and exporting, virtually cutting themselves off from the rest of the world. They found, over time, that without taking in broader thought and the community of the world (that includes customers and vendors and supporters) they simply couldn't sustain their business and growth the way they anticipated. This doesn't just happen in capitalistic societies. We see it all over the world and at every level at any given point in history.

In this book, and through a more thorough look at the detriment this defined growth mindset can have on a business, more of us will exchange a growth mindset for a betterment mindset, thus paving the way for real sustainable growth, personal success and creation of a larger community that will forever support the business.

Imagine a society that truly embraced the idea of creating a better environment, better systems and better services and products. Imagine a level of accountability among each of the members to contribute something back to that society.

As we take a look around our world, with all of its conflicts and divisions in thoughts and yes, even truths, the idea of only focusing on what the paper says and not understanding the why and the how and the impact on self and society, will create the fall of the growth mindset.

You'll see the fall of the growth mindset as you journey forward into this idea of business betterment. Your actions will become more mindful and purposeful, not to mention filled with sincerity that customers and team members will notice.

The opportunities are endless with a business betterment mindset!

3. GROWTH VS BETTERMENT MINDSET

The Growth Mindset Versus the Betterment Mindset, Defined

This is where we dive in to really comparing the definitions of the growth and betterment mindsets, side-by-side, for each area of business that we will cover in this book.

What this comparison allows you and your company to do is see the differences in the thought process as it pertains to each area of impact to your business. You will easily be able to see where in your business the growth mindset or the betterment mindset is being used, which allows you to see gaps in your company that you may not have seen before considering this way of thinking. It is the first step in creating the betterment mindset from a place of authentic conversations and information. This is the start of a process you can not un-know. You can never go back to being in a state of complete unawareness when it comes to your business. And then you must make a decision, do you take the blue pill? Or the red pill?

Operations

The operations area of our business is really one of the most central components of how and where the wheels turn that make the whole process of getting from A to B possible. It is the area where many key daily activities start such as budgeting, labor, processes for implementation of sales, and marketing. And, importantly, is often the starting point for communication in your supply chain.

Betterment Operations

We define operations within this mindset as the logistical, administrative and key activities that internally produce your products and services in a way that best serves the team, customer, business and community.

Growth Operations

We define operations within the growth mindset as all activities to produce a product or service as efficiently as possible for as little cost as possible.

The difference here is clear. The betterment mindset is based on inclusion and the concept of "doing the right thing." It is based on making decisions utilizing all the information obtained, including the budget numbers, quantifying efficiency, and making decisions that are best for the customer, the business and the community.

The growth mindset is not based on authentic communication between the various areas of a business. In this mindset, operations dictates direction based on decisions made in a vacuum and on a spreadsheet with very little interaction between all parties who are affected by the operations of a business.

Products And Services (P&S)

This is the heart of our business. This is our identity, our area of expertise and our area of passion. It is the "what" of what we bring to the table that has the potential of changing lives.

Betterment P&S

The betterment mindset defines products and services as the key value your company creates, packages and sells that solves, with passion, a need or want in the world.

Growth P&S

The growth mindset defines products and services as those things that create revenue streams that provide the highest possible profit margin.

Again, the differences between these mindsets are clear. The betterment mindset comes from a place of authenticity of creating a solution that will have a positive impact on the lives of customers. While the products and services under the definition of the growth mindset *may* also do that, the decisions of which products and services to offer come from one place only: which products and services can be produced with the highest profit margins, not necessarily those products that are the best for the customer, but the ones that will either have the highest return on investment (ROI) because of the lowest expense margin or highest price point or a mass selling appeal. None of these ROI's are bad, they are the opposite, in fact. But they are only truly good if they don't blatantly disregard the other important aspects that we have mentioned in the definition of betterment products and services.

Leadership

A strong leadership in a business is one that drives the mission and the values of the company. Leaders are not always the ones in the top seat of a business, but are seen at each and every level. Leaders set the example of integrity in a business as seen in decision making, attitude, behavior, and action.

Betterment Leadership

Leadership as defined under the betterment mindset are those strategic activities that navigate the direction of the organization at every level.

Growth Leadership

The growth mindset defines leadership as top-down decision making that controls the direction of the company.

With the business betterment mindset, leadership comes from a "we're all in this together" mindset which creates authentic and transparent buy-in, sharing of information, a culture that is defined by perception, and executed activities that reflect the values of the business. Leadership in a growth mindset environment is based on a dictation of culture based on a "we know best" mentality, operating under "because we said so" and is not fully inclusive of all team members and areas of the business if it does not serve its higher level decision makers purpose.

Management

Especially in mid-size to larger businesses, an infrastructure that includes management positions needs to exist in order to create a point of communication, leadership and decision making that allows an organization to flow smoothly with defined roles.

Betterment Management

Management defined under the betterment mindset is the inclusive oversight of resource and activity execution for furthering company objectives.

Growth Management

The growth mindset definition for management is the top-down decision making that controls the direction of the resources.

If you look at both of these definitions, you will see the glaring difference in the words used: inclusive for betterment and control for growth. The betterment mindset "rallies the troops", while the growth mindset is focused on more of a dictatorial approach to management. You will notice that the management and leadership definitions are very similar for the growth mindset. That is because in many corporations the people within the organization and running the organization don't see much of a difference, if a difference at all, between management and leadership. They believe their leaders are the managers and their managers are the leaders.

Team

A solid team is an integral part of any business. These are the resources that support you, sell your products, preach the values and messages of your business along with giving you balance inside and outside of the business.

Betterment Team

All of the people who support the fulfillment of your products and services are a part of a betterment mentality business team. This includes all independent contractors, suppliers, wholesale and influencers.

Growth Team

Human resources used to further your company's bottom line are what define those involved in a business currently practicing within the growth mindset.

Again, as in leadership, the growth mindset promotes more of an exclusionary approach to the ability to reach business objectives and does not consider the importance of creating a structure that embraces and promotes transparency and authentic conversation.

Culture

Culture is the unwritten perception of what our business stands for as it relates to the stated mission and values. The value of culture is that it goes a long way when it comes to attracting like-minded team members, building loyalty among customers and creating trust in a community.

Betterment Culture

The feeling and perception people get when thinking about their experience with your company is how culture is defined within the business betterment mindset.

Growth Culture

Culture in this mindset is a defined company policy and logic used to mold team members to a specific mindset and way of being.

Culture can only be determined by an authentic reaction from anyone who interacts with a business. It is not something that should, or could, ever truly be controled or dictated, as the growth mindset definition suggests.

This can breed resentment and fear among team members, customers and even the community as it doesn't honestly match with activities. Culture is set by actions, not as defined by policy because that is something one "hopes" the culture is.

Marketing

Marketing sets the stage for sales to happen. The marketing team, based on input from sales and product development, creates messaging that will enable the sales team to work with customers on closing the sale of a product or service. Marketing also uses feedback to create a brand identity from the words used to the images conveyed and even packaging of products and services.

Betterment Marketing

Marketing under the betterment mindset definition uses the brand and personality for creation of conversation and public consumption. It does so to build interest and awareness.

Growth Marketing

In the growth mindset world, marketing is a medium to talk to the world to convince or plant the seed that a person or group needs a particular product or service.

In this mindset, marketing is often viewed as an expense line item that is disposable. However, the primary difference between these two mindsets when it comes to marketing is once again in the inclusionary and authentic approach. Within the betterment mindset, marketing relies on communication with and among the various areas of the business including the customers and community. In the growth mindset, marketing is solely focused on the quantity of the information used to attract customers in any fashion necessary to create the sale.

Sales

Sales is what turns the products and services into revenue for a business. The sales team is the front line, along with customer service, when it comes to interacting with the community and with customers. One of their purposes is to build relationships and encourage conversation with the public and potential customers.

Betterment Sales

As defined in the betterment mindset, sales is all the activities that happen after someone knows your company exists and are interested in exploring how your products and services can be of value to a group or individual.

Growth Sales

In the growth mindset, sales is revenue focused activity to convince people to purchase your product or service.

While revenue focused activities are obviously important to the success of a business and also dictates the desirability of the products and services to customers, the key difference is in the approach itself. Sales should be an ongoing process to employ customer loyalty and trust in the product or service itself. Having a revenue-only focused approach to sales runs the risk of one-offs in product sales, higher customer turnover and an over-all negative customer perception of your company, even if it is a commodity or product that they need. The moment someone does it better or differently, they will leave your company's products or services because they were not comfortable with buying them in the first place even though they felt they needed them because of price or functionality or clever fear-based marketing.

Customer Experience (C E)

The customer experience with your products, services and processes along with your business as a whole dictates what kind of reputation you have with customers and the community. Customer experience can only be determined by asking for (and if you are lucky) receiving and then accepting completely honest feedback.

Betterment CE

With the betterment mindset, customer experience is defined as all of the interaction your company has with people who resonate with your product or services.

Growth CE

Customer experience defined in the growth mindset is a management of customer expectations.

The primary difference between these two mindsets is the betterment mindset sets the stage for transparency and the ability to create an even better experience, face challenges and build strong relationships based on the continuous interactions and requests for feedback. It takes courage company wide to show the vulnerable side of your business as you take in feedback and work to strengthen your relationships with the public.

One's Own

Your own mindset is key in how you approach and respond to day-to-day business activities, challenges, family and just life in general. It is how you prioritize, balance and plan in a way where you can take decisive action and be flexible with lifes ever changing challenges in and out of the office.

Betterment in One's Own

The betterment mindset defines one's own as a mindset used to navigate the different rules and hats worn outside of work that impact your career, health, happiness, wealth and fulfillment and continually move forward with those aspects of life.

Growth in One's Own

The definition under the traditional growth mindset is work as much as you can for as long as you can to create a safety net. Then, at the end of it all, enjoying life is a luxury and reward for the hard work you put in on the front end.

The difference between the two mindsets is the focus

on balance. Without balance we run the risk of burn-out, resentment and feelings of discontentment. In the growth mindset we often hear about work/life balance, but often it is spoken of with empty promises and resentment when personal time or focus on health and family is taken, even to a reasonable amount. We believe that someone with a pure growth mindset would conceptually agree with our One's Own processes, but in execution would show anything but agreeance. And as we know, actions speak louder than words.

◆ ◆ ◆

There are two more terms we want to define while we are at it, as we will be using them quite often. We may elaborate on these concepts further throughout the book, but we wanted to get a head start.

Authenticity

Genuine. Original. Accurate. Reliable. Authenticity is all of these things. It is operating in a way where you know and understand who your company is at its core and can communicate that effectively through your company's actions. Your company doesn't try to mimic or copy other company's. Your leadership and your management is comfortable with who your company is and portrays that without any misleading filters.

Transparency

Easily perceived and understood. Transparency means

your company is in plain sight. There is nothing happening that your mom would be ashamed of. Nothing is being intentionally controlled or hidden out of fear or greed. Everything within the organization is accessible, within reason of security and protection of intellectual property, sensitive employee and customer information and the like.

These are the definitions of each area of business we will be covering in this book, as seen by both mindsets. You may agree with the betterment mindset definitions. You may agree with the growth mindset definitions. You may at times agree with both. This is totally normal. Especially because some of the growth mindset definitions focus on important things. However, it doesn't focus holistically on all of the fundamentally right things.

Also note that we are talking about two ends of a spectrum. And most businesses are somewhere in between a complete betterment mindset and complete growth mindset. You may be able to see both mindsets appear in the same business, but how aligned they are with either one on an average tells you more about a business than an individually observed action.

The betterment mindset does not compromise on the strengths of the growth mindset. It doesn't ask companies to be non-profits or sacrifice themselves for the greater good. As you will see in the chapters to come, it simply asks that we as business owners, employees and board members do the right things and we do them well. It's simple, but not always easy. But as we have seen in countless businesses, often doing what is easy is not doing what is best and costs reputation and business in the long run far more than the short term gain it may provide.

4. MOVING FORWARD WITH BETTERMENT

Moving Forward with Betterment

Moving forward with the betterment mindset can be beneficial at every level of business. Every decision made, whether as a part of the growth mindset or the betterment mindset, has an impact on the business, regardless of the size. Each type of business, like everything in life, has its strengths and weaknesses that lend to growth opportunities. Some things in this book will be easier for larger businesses to understand and implement. Some parts of this book will be easier for smaller businesses to utilize and implement. All of it is usable if framed with the right decision making and strategic processes. That is the Business Betterment Model at its finest.

When we all feel as though we are truly a part of something bigger, when we know we have some skin in the game, it can change our entire outlook on business, our professional lives and our society.

When you are looking at what to do next with your business to "take it to the next level," what do you do first? Do you go to your spreadsheets and find the deficits and view those as opportunities? Do you automatically look at all of the numbers such as sales numbers or expense numbers first? What if you were to take the time and really reflect on what it is about your business that satisfies you and your customers the most? Could you do more of that? Are those possible next steps the reason you got into the business that you are in today?

When the customer feels noticed and "heard" you are on your way to creating a much deeper relationship and an intrinsic loyalty with that customer. What happens next? Well, you see your referrals go up, your sales go up and your efforts to retain customers become easier.

These are some of the first steps to joining the Business Betterment Movement and it applies to businesses of all sizes. In this chapter we're going to dive into the initial thought process to start moving forward in the betterment mindset.

This thought process is merely the beginning of taking the journey towards business betterment. It is the beginning of a reconnection with yourself, your team and your business as a whole. And, as you reconnect with your business, you will begin to gain additional insight into what the next steps for you and your business is and so will start the path of business betterment.

You will also find that reconnecting with your own team as well as your family and community, in ways that may seem new to you, will not only strengthen relationships but will also have the byproduct of the creation of a better and stronger business.

And so begins the betterment mindset. It's creating a meaningful experience with purpose.

How do you begin? The first step in your journey to a betterment mindset is to first commit to taking the deep dive into understanding what your business values truly are and what you are willing to do to achieve those goals for your customers and communities.

Where do you authentically see your business (and yourself) in 5 years? In 10 years? These questions are not to promote worry about the future, but rather to instill a thought process. A process that, while living and working in the moment, will lend a better understanding of your own thought process and character. Your thought process and character is then injected in and is reflected through your business and, most importantly, your actions.

Write your thoughts down throughout this book. You can then see a shift in your thought process as you go along. This very well could be the first step to creating a healthier business, a healthier life and a healthier mind that you have been looking for.

Now, what are you willing to do to achieve those goals? In other words, if you want to double your sales, are you willing to put in the amount of time it likely will take to do so? What sacrifices are you willing to make? Go deep. Really think about all aspects of your business that will be impacted, and how, with this type of mindset it might be impacted. Consider why and what consequences it will have on your business, your team, and your community when you think about doubling your sales, not just how. The "why" will help you, your business and your team understand what is important, what is a priority and what it will take both personally and professionally. And it will help you understand the accountability and commitment necessary to get there.

There are no wrong answers here at all. Getting into the betterment mindset means knowing that the path you are on is the right one for you. It's a lot easier to be committed that way!

Identify the gaps in where you are in your business and personal life with where you want to be. What are the challenges you face in order to close those gaps?

Look at the big picture. Where do you see yourself when it comes to being a part of something? A part of the community? A part of the bigger picture? Does it involve volunteering for a cause or giving back in some other way? Maybe it's making time to coach your kids sports teams or have a schedule and situation that allows for frequent vacations and time with family and friends.

What role do you want to play in society? How do you see yourself giving back? As a part of the Betterment Movement, we also strive to help others join the movement as well. We strive to give back in ways that improve our society, ourselves and those around us.

What Size Is Your Business?

The betterment mindset does have a different effect among different sizes of business. So let's talk about.

Small Business

In a small business of five employees, or even less, the move to business betterment is one that will create not only sustainability but will also have a profoundly positive impact on the business owner as well as the team. It doesn't necessarily have to take resources to join the business betterment movement, but rather it's a large shift in attitude. Therefore, even in an environment of just a handful of people, it's not only possible, but essential.

While small businesses certainly would not be in a position to provide the same level of financial support to the local community as a larger business, their contribution is extremely important and the importance for sustainability is to follow the betterment business model.

Small businesses surely struggle in a different way, generally with a different level of resources, but that struggle will only grow and continue to ultimate deterioration if the only mindset is a growth mindset. Creating broader thought and balance will ultimately create sustainability for the business and the people within.

Within the walls of a small business, with less than five employees, it's even more critical to avoid becoming isolated. There seems to be a tendency to get caught up in the daily grind, so to speak, which creates an even bigger chance to fall into that growth only mindset. It is much easier to get bogged down in the crises that seem to dominate our days.

Focus on business culture and community comes about in many ways. As a small business owner, with a team of five or less, you have the opportunity of a great interpersonal sounding board for new ideas. These ideas can contribute to operation efficiency, marketing and promotion, what customers are saying, and how to engage with the community. And this holds true even if you are a one-person show, you do have a business culture that is perceived by those around you and driven by your actions. It just may take a bit more creativity in terms of having a sounding board. Getting a coach or someone you know that always helps get your creative mind flowing would be a great idea!

Involving each of your team members in a small office environment allows you to carve out additional time for yourself to create opportunities for business strategy thought, as well as that very much needed time for life-work balance. How does this work? Engaging your team members in this process gives them the opportunity to accept accountability and feel included in the success of the business. It is a step towards a "we're all in this together" mentality that people tend to crave when they become part of a business vision and mission.

Creating a culture around this involvement also creates a culture of trust, one of the much needed foundations for sustainability and business betterment. While this may be true of any size office, it is very evident even more quickly evident in smaller businesses.

As you read through this book, you will learn more about specific ways to implement this idea of business betterment into your daily life. We've seen businesses this size actually increase their bottom line in a more sustainable and healthy manner by better understanding the very delicate culture in a small office, creating boundaries with each other and customers, taking time for much needed and re-energizing self-care.

Mid-Size Business

When you have a business that's slightly larger, say 20 to 30 employees, it's equally as important to engage and fully communicate with everyone as with a small business. That sense of belonging is so important to us as human beings and translates directly to creating sustainability in business. And, with a few more team members, that isolation and "tribalism" can happen very quickly.

In this size of business, the practice of business betterment is most often noticeable in the success of the business culture with a high level of inclusion among team members. Input is not only solicited from each team member, but it is valued and incorporated often into new products and processes. Other than the complexity of team and culture changing and spending more energy learning how to meet demand through different distribution chains, many of the struggles will be similar to smaller businesses and some hybrid challenges from larger businesses.

Large Businesses, government funded entities and publicly traded corporations

Larger businesses and corporations have discovered this idea of business betterment in many ways. This is primarily due to pressure from consumers and a need to adapt because of how every decision made in a large organization can significantly impact a community or even our global health.

Think about the ways that many large businesses provide support to local cities and communities. Many of them have gone as far as providing funding for transitional housing and even daycare services to help those needing a leg up.

This kind of broader thought not only follows the business betterment movement by recognizing the need to address long term needs of a community that will ultimately provide a stronger foundation, but it also creates a reach that goes far beyond the bottom line.

While not all of this is philanthropic, consumers have become very aware of when a company is doing good because it meshes well with their brand and mission as a capitalistic organization but also does good for the global community, or when it is a PR ploy to try to boost their image by less-than-aware consumers.

The most difficult aspect of incorporating the betterment mindset is how slow change can spread through larger organizations. Not to mention, how much effort and expense some changes way make if they are incredibly far down the rabbithole of the growth mindset. Also, depending on the position of the individual reading this book, there may not feel like there is a lot of power or influence that can be had on the overall organization.

What we have found with micro-influencers, new employees or hands-on workers is that they can execute a lot of these betterment mindset rules in their immediate workplace. Change, growth and efficiency gets noticed and with the numbers speaking for themselves, larger company leaders and influencers are more open and receptive. Keep fighting the good fight!

Moving Forward

This idea of authenticity and collaboration is not a new idea. We've been talking about it for quite some time now in different contexts as a society. Mostly those conversations have been focused on a specific issue and not comprehensive. This book is here to change that.

And, it's having those conversations with authenticity and collaboration. It's not about how it all looks on paper behind closed doors.

When this true sincerity and clarity penetrates an organization, it literally transcends to the end user, the customer.

Throughout this book, we'll take you along the journey of business discovery, self-discovery, process-discovery and customer discovery to prepare you to take your business and you to the next level and beyond. And, the great news is that you're going to do it all with your own goals and personal life balance in mind. Nothing should feel forced, unattainable, or unimplementable. It's time to get back to doing what's right for ourselves which actually transcends to doing what's right for our families and our businesses.

It's time to join the Business Betterment Movement.

PART 2

The Betterment Model

5. BETTERMENT OPERATIONS

I f you have decided to take the steps and join the betterment business movement, be prepared to watch your business grow in deep ways that you may not have even imagined were possible.

Why is this? Because as you begin to and continue to focus on the betterment mindset with your business, with the right team and right tools that lead your company towards transparency and authenticity, you will attract those clients, customers, team members and colleagues that want to be a part of what you have created. What transpires is a redefined growth.

Honestly, businesses that have nailed their products and services are not likely prepared for this redefined growth that we are talking about in this book. More often than not this inability to react to sustainable growth is due to systems, policies and procedures that aren't setup to sustain the growth spurts. Growth spurts can hurt because of the gap in logistical or human resources between the current level of success and the one your customers are pushing you towards.

Let's look at what the betterment of your business operations can look like under a betterment mindset, and how it can help you focus your operations and future-proof them for growth, depressions, market booms, pandemics, natural disasters and anything else the world can throw at you.

Betterment Operation Definition

As a part of the betterment mindset, we define the operations of a business as the logistical, administrative, and key activities that internally produce your products and/or services that best serve your team, customer and community.

Operations can mean many different things depending on the perspective of the business or the person involved in the various aspects of the business. From an ecological perspective, the creation and distribution of products that expanded exponentially during the industrial revolution was the single biggest detriment our planet has ever experienced. From an innovation perspective, the industrial and technological advancements humankind has made through business activity are truly magnificent. From an employee perspective, the working conditions most of our ancestors have had to endure and that globally continue to occur are ridiculous and inhumane. From a customer perspective, the ability to acquire almost anything you want for a lower value cost than ever before is beyond empowering.

With all of these perspectives being valid, the question is clear: knowing that products and services will continue to exist as long as human needs and wants do, how can we limit the negative impact of operations? Furthermore, how can we do so while continuing to improve the human experience around the world? It starts with one business at a time and with a betterment mindset.

In this chapter we outline the five rules your company can follow to optimally answer that very question as well as be aligned with the betterment model of business.

Rule #1: Slow, Continuous Improvement Over A Long Period Of Time Is The Best Approach To Operations.

This rule is proven time and time again, not only in a business environment but in our personal lifestyles and health.

The question, "how can we do "X" better than we currently are?"

If your interested in the origination of this principle, Google Kaizen. The first rule of Betterment Operations is the literal definition of this. It is a philosophy that was articulated by Japanese organizational theorist Masaaki Imai. The most interesting aspect of this betterment rule isn't that it is groundbreaking as a concept, but it is remarkable that it is actually incredibly well received in the operations community that is purely focused on the bottom-line and efficiency. Even margin-pinching businesses have seen the value and profitability of focusing on the improvement of various areas of business operations over time, so as not to drive too much global stress and change at once.

However, some businesses, small and large, miss the mark. Be careful that, as a part of the planning process, improvement doesn't become wrongly defined. Improvement is the improvement of quality, working conditions, distribution efficiency, vendor relationships and process improvement. All of these aspects are vital to overall sustainability.

Note also that this rule can be applied to an entire business, not just its logistics and product fulfillment. The key word here is improvement. And it isn't improvement in extreme, short bursts. Improvement becomes a part of the product life cycle. It is incorporated and understood to be valuable when it stands alone and as its own procedure and business function. Improvement isn't a response to an issue. It is proactive, flowing, and continuous.

Another benefit to making smaller changes over time is that the effectiveness of the change can be more easily tracked. If a business changes too many things too quickly, whether the business starts doing better or worse it is nearly impossible to see what changes are having what effect on the business. And if a business doesn't know what makes it better or worse, it can hardly improve from tangible, purposeful action. Let alone have rapid success.

Even what people consider "rapid" success doesn't happen overnight. By rapid success we mean when we treat the symptoms rather than address core issues and needs for the purpose of seeing quick, but short-lived successful results. Even if it did work well in the long run, it would be the result of years of groundwork that laid the way for it to happen.

A lot of businesses make big "pushes" such as one-time initiatives to change up processes in the hopes of creating improvement. There is nothing wrong with this inherently, if the systems and processes and operations remain consistent in between these pushes. But what happens to most businesses and their team is they burn out after these pushes, causing a recession in continuous movement of the business.

Build slow, don't let being in a hurry lead to critical mistakes or inaccurate ability to report. Patience is key to continuous improvement. But, don't move too slow. as soon as you stop making progress, your business starts decaying.

Rule #2: If You Are Focused On Betterment, You Must Plan For Growth.

And, under the business betterment mindset, this growth that we plan for is redefined into a deeper and more sustainable growth.

A business that is filling a need or want in the world and doing it well will grow and experience success at some point. Whether or not they hit bankruptcy before that point based on funding or poor business practices is a different topic. If your business is focused on betterment, you will find success sooner rather than later. And, as we've said, betterment leads to growth.

Planning for this growth can be the difference between being able to hold the weight of demand or to be crushed by it. If the systems, processes, policies and procedures are not ready to handle the growth in a business it can lead to higher costs, stunted growth, employee frustration, customer frustration, bad customer service, tainted reputation and loss of trust of vendors and other inefficiencies.

In summation that means making your administrative and product operations scaleable for growth. This will allow your company to ride the growth wave instead of being thrown under the riptide and being rolled through the reefs. Some of the features of betterment operations include:

Systems, policies and procedures that are easily usable and easily communicated for every action required to fulfill your products and services.

Knowing and correctly utilizing the capacity of your resources, facilities and operations team.

Having a plan for growing 25%, 50%, 100%.

Also have a plan for a decrease of sales up to 50%.

These are especially critical in times like we are seeing currently with the unknown economic climate due to being in the middle of a pandemic.

That last point may surprise you, but because we have no idea what industry you are in it needs to be acknowledged that some industries are very volatile and have very drastic differences in yearly gross income. If you are always planning and operating off of your best year or best possible year, it doesn't leave room for error in the years that will, at some point, be a bit more of a struggle than others.

Ultimately, anything to answer the question, "What do we have to do to prepare for growth and what will that allow our business to accomplish next?" or "What do we have to do to prepare for a mild to moderate recession of business?" becomes a part of your growth plan because it is a part of your betterment plan.

Rule #3: The Main Focus Of Operations Is The Quality And Perfected Execution Of Products And Services With As Little Negative Environmental And Community Impact As Possible. This Is What We Call Operative Responsibility.

When producing a product, there will be an environmental impact on some level. This idea is difficult to come to terms with for eco-minded companies. Luckily, there are many things that can be done to negate and minimize the footprint left from productions. Operations is a balancing act in determining what can be done, and the cost feasibility of your efforts for sustainability. No one is perfect (i.e no one composts *all* of their waste and no one gets *every* single piece of plastic in their necessary bin) but with the mindset of operations betterment rule #1, the growth and betterment of your company will be a positive successful upward spiral.

Let's look at how this rule applies when looking at business operations that focus on outsourcing for betterment. Betterment businesses do not outsource without first looking at the environmental and community impact of this decision. There is clearly a benefit to working with different countries who have different strengths and contributions to the world. But to simply do it "cheaper" without knowing the consequences of this one criteria (cost), after all that we have learned about the environmental impact and unequivocal labor practices, is not business savviness but laziness and greed. These are not qualities of a better business. We aren't saying outsourcing is a bad thing. We are just saying most companies do it without looking at important betterment variables.

In fact, we have seen businesses take the time and energy to invest in finding the perfect partners for outsourcing and actually save revenue over the alternatives that simply sought outsourcing with the intent on finding the lowest price possible. The shift in perception to betterment led to different parameters for searching that aren't even on most businesses radars. More business relationships led to reaching different markets and not having to go through the vendor contracting process when something inevitably didn't work out. They saved the expense of customer service on faulty products not produced well and on lawsuit payouts for situations that arise from product failure.

Your businesses may not be at a high level of production, but every action still has an equal and opposite reaction in your bottom line, your customer perception, your employee satisfaction and productivity.

When providing a service, the standard at which you provide it is a crucial aspect of your company's reputation. The service process is your value proposition and without a process and challenge of continuously focusing on the quality and perfected execution, your customers will find gaps in the service. In most situations, if this lack of attention to betterment is not remedied, loyal customers will eventually find a competitor that fills those gaps and raises the bar, even at a premium cost.

Rule #4: The Secondary Focus Of Operations Is Always Customer And Employee Experience.

Even though customer experience and team are their own betterment chapters, they are the reason that operations exist and this needs to be factored into the management and leadership decision making processes of the operations departments.

While the main focus is on perfecting the product and service, focusing on how they are being used by customers will feed your company insights on how to fulfill Operation Betterment Rule #3 even better. What you and your team think is internally better for a product or service may not be received with the same enthusiasm. If you can find a way to seamlessly include your customers in the operations process by giving valuable feedback, do it.

By focusing on what the customer wants through the operation processes, and by asking them whenever possible what they want and need, your operations will continuously reach a new level of success.

In terms of employees, there is nothing more important in operations (other than quality products and services) than employee satisfaction. The working conditions in your administrative and operational locations are imperative to retention and improvement. Happy

Employee. Happy Customer. Happy Bottom-Line.

Additionally, employees are essentially internal customers. If they believe in the business and the business model, and they have a use for it, they are probably utilizing your products or services to some extent. They are also telling people about them continuously both inside and outside the business. If given the chance and not reprimanded for it, they will be brutally honest about what can be done better. Creating a transparent environment and correctly leveraging it is an advanced and complex betterment secret that hardly any business has successfully mastered.

Rule #5: Operations' Final Focus Is Cost, Compliance And Communication Between The Various Areas And Departments In A Business.

We understand that cost is important, but quality, employee satisfaction, and customer satisfaction (without breaking the bank) are far more important to sustainability and growth. Cost does need to be factored in and this is something that comes inherent to most business planning departments and managers so we don't need to say too much here.

Additionally, ensuring the highest levels of compliance that are applicable can be a marketing tool for those who need an extra layer of trust and risk-aversion reassurance have it before purchasing your products and services.

Finally, having a process and dedication within the operation department to effectively communicate with other departments will put your business above and beyond because there is an anticipated and expected, welcome openness. One of the biggest interdepartmental frustrations is not understanding or not being included properly in operational communications. This leads to broken customer service which leads to a negative customer experience and stressed employees who have to cover for operations for reasons that could be easily remedied by holding operational employees to a higher communication standard.

These are the five betterment rules for operations in your business. The more of these your company is following and implementing, the more sustainable growth your business will experience. Maybe this is an oversimplification but if you take nothing else away from this chapter remember this; Do not cut corners, do not mistreat employees, and do not deceive or short-hand customers. Okay, okay. Here's a positive reframe: Put quality first, go above and beyond for your employees, and create the best customer experience possible. Always.

6. BETTERMENT PRODUCTS AND SERVICES

Our products and services are the bread and butter of our business. Simply put, in order to pay our bills, we have to engage with the right customers that will result in an exchange of service or product for revenue.

When you think about the products and services that you offer, what comes to mind first? Do you initially think about the cleverness of the product, what it does specifically? Do you think about how great your service is, how unique or different you are than others? Do you think back to the inception of the idea of the product or services?

If this is what you think of first when it comes to your products and services, we are going to challenge that thinking on the way to business betterment.

What if you instead looked at your products and services and asked this question first: How does my product or service contribute in such a way that adds value to others? How does my product or service change the lives of others?

Could you answer those question fully and openly and with authenticity?

When you developed your products and services, what did you see as the purpose? Was it to provide a solution for yourself where you felt others could also find benefit? Did you ask yourself, "what keeps my prospective customers up at night?" And, "can I provide a solution that enhances their lives?"

Most of us went into business because we felt that what we had to offer would provide benefit to others. If you are working for a business, the founders probably started from this same foundation. But how did we come to that determination? What made us so sure that we were adding value and changing lives?

As you take the journey towards business betterment, get reacquainted with becoming a part of the solution. I know you might be surprised, but it's incredible how many businesses truly miss the mark when it comes to truly providing something their customers are asking for and are craving, especially as time passes and customers evolve from when the business first opened. When you don't consider the specific contribution that you are able to make with your products and services, it can land you in a position of having a poor reputation or little integrity, which translates to no customer loyalty. Think of it this way; if you go beyond treating the symptoms and help others find real solutions to whatever challenges they face, you are adding value and changing lives.

In order to rise above this caliber of business, your business must align with the following betterment rules for products and services:

Rule #1: Compete On Quality And Service, Not Cost.

Unless your business is the likes of Walmart, there's no need (or even sustainable possibility) to compete on price. Depending on what your product or service is, if you focus only on price, you could set yourself up for creating a commodity, which ultimately depends on price. Those are the only two exceptions to the rule of the focus on cost before anything else.

If you compete on cost, you are always going to end up either driving away your best customers, best employees or both. That isn't to say that you don't want to price effectively. But just setting price based on other businesses norms or a blanket norm in your industry isn't taking into account your unique set of expenses and opportunity costs. Set prices by taking into consideration your business' own uniqueness, reputation, and purpose.

Competing on quality means you are not making any sacrifices on the actual integrity of your service or product simply for the sake of pricing to sell more. No business makes a product or service quite like yours, at quite the level or with quite the same perspective. Honestly most similar products can't even be compared effectively because of the hundreds of factors that make the businesses different. And while supply, demand, economics and statistics can give us insights into the workings of an industry and its pricing structure, it cannot predict what we should charge.

The best way to compete on quality and to acknowledge the price you have set is to have a solid, tangible formula for calculating value. This will ensure you can justify it to any decision makers and even use some of the competitive advantage points as marketing material.

Competing on service means making sure that your company treats your customers and even your employees better than any other competitive presence. What "treats better" means varies greatly to each industry and even to each customer. However, the process that your customers go through can be the difference in how your customers are willing to pay higher prices or not. Even for sometimes inferior products and services. You can better understand this by better engaging in conversation with your customer. Or, you can see this displayed in the example below.

Here is a situation for you to ponder. There are two tire replacement service companies. Company one sells tires that are 30% better quality than its competitor, but the waiting facility is incredibly dirty, there is nowhere to sit and wait for the service to be completed and the employees are dismissive and doing their bare minimum. After your car is finished and returned to you, you get on the highway. The driving seems a bit wobbly and off which is concerning, so you pull over and give them a call. No one answers the phone. You try again, nothing. Come to think of it, they never answer the phone when you call. You've always had to physically go there to schedule your services. So you turn around and return to the service facility. You approach the front to ask a question and your inquiry is received with eye rolls and condescending remarks. You ask to speak to the manager, only to be received with the same attitude and irritation. It seems like you must be a burden to them and they are too busy to have time for your "issue". They reluctantly take it back to look at it. It takes another hour, and they charge an hour's labor to tighten the lug nuts one of their service members forgot to tighten for the service you already paid for. The total cost is around $300, which, with the extra time and screw up, is still marginally less than the average competitor.

Company two's tires may not be as high of quality, but they have no real complaints from manufacture, warranty or driver issues. However, their waiting area feels luxurious. They have amenities such coffee, tea, snacks, magazines, television, and even a community puzzle on the coffee table. It's oddly clean for how dirty the service workers are that you can see working on vehicles through their glass service viewing windows. The staff is incredibly friendly and always remembers your name and situations you mentioned, even from six months ago. The owner/manager knows you by name as well and always sits with you to explain how long it will take and the specifics of the tire service. You get a courtesy call after thanking you for your business and asking if there is anything they could do better. If you ever have any issues they are always incredibly responsive and get you in right away as if you are their only customer. Fully warrantied, no charge or questions ask. You and your family even get a small gift basket during the holiday season as a thank you for being a customer. Your usual cost is around $375 for the same service as their competitor.

Which business do you think is doing better? Which business do you think *should* be doing better? Which business would you bring your car for service?

If you would usually stick with company one, you are in a rare percentage of people who buy solely and completely on price. The vast majority of us have more emotional stake in businesses that invest their time and energy in us and will even compromise quality for service *and* pay a higher price for it.

This isn't to say that the majority of us don't look for the best value, and we are more than likely willing to settle on some moral and conveniences for a lower price, but not the bottom of the barrel.

As long as the company stays in business, one could argue that neither of these companies are "wrong" or "bad" in their business model. The difference here is a company that believes solely that the only way to compete is low cost, regardless of service and the other believes that reasonable costs allow for better company and customer culture without taking advantage or cutting corners.

Just some food for thought!

Rule #2: Become A Part Of The Solution.

Truly beneficial products always solve an issue or challenge for the customer and ultimately even the community in some way. These products and services generally get to the root cause of a community situation and seek to remedy it from its deepest level.

As defined by the betterment mindset, products and services are the key values your company creates, packages and sells that solves, with passion, a need or want in the world. These products and services are executed with the customers' needs at the forefront driving most of the decisions associated with those products and services.

This differs from the exclusive growth mindset which defines products and services as those things that create revenue streams that provide the highest possible profit margin. The focus here is delivery based on cost and the cost of delivering those products and services.

You will be amazed how much sustainable growth is possible by simply putting yourself in your customers' shoes first. Most businesses do this naturally but lose sight of the solution they thought to provide by getting lost in the numbers. We all have needs. We all have wants. Most of us don't have a perfect solution yet for every product and service in our life. By finding and being that solution, you offer hope and possibility and excitement to those who want to keep moving forward in whatever capacity they determine as success.

So, How does your product or service help others? How are you a contributor to society? And who benefits (other than you) from this product or service?

Rule #3: Realistically Promise, Over Deliver.

I'm sure you have heard the phrase "under promise, over deliver." However, under promising is still a deceit in order to gain customer praise. Products and services should always accurately represent their actual benefit. With the realistic understanding that there is no magical pill.

From a place of actual benefit, you can provide additional benefits that customers don't fully know or aren't fully aware of until they experience your product or service. And their experience of those benefits may vary from customer to customer. Most customers seek their primary benefit but, as we know, our products, services, and customer service features can be more complex than what meets the eye at first glance. With these additional benefits, delivered over time, we can begin to unveil the true benefits of our products and services and our company. This is what we mean by realistically promise, and then it is also okay to over-deliver.

Products and services should always accurately represent their actual benefit. Try to never over promise or under deliver. And, along those lines, always be honest and transparent about what your product or service can or cannot do. The worst situation to find yourself in is trying to explain your way out of an indiscretion or perceived indiscretion to your customers. Be upfront and authentic with your customers and your team about your products and services and their actual capabilities. If you are approaching your products and services from a betterment mindset, this won't be an issue as you will continuously be engaging with your team and your customers and delivering from a place of passion and intent.

Rule #4: The Best Products And Services Start With A Smart Product And Service Development Process.

Establish or refine your product development process to take the time to flush out ideas, test solutions with customers, and plan your execution. Having a major oversight of a product after creating and distributing them is a huge nightmare. This can and has "killed" start-ups who are swimming in debt and are launching their first product or service too prematurely. Take the time to do it right from the very beginning.

There is something that can be slightly less obvious but equally costly in the long run: efficiency leaks. Having minor efficiency leaks in one or more parts of the product or service delivery cycles can add up astoundingly in the long run. These expense leaks usually happen because of something that has been ill planned in the development process.

Let's take a simple service example; let's say that a law firm is planning to add a new service to their law service offerings. They fulfill all of the planning involved in getting the service launched and executed. However, there is a document that they could have created that is a complete template to walk a client through the new process step by step to get all of the information they need up front. They didn't think to do this. Therefore, the attorney responsible for meeting with new clients usually has to prep for 30 minutes more before a new client meeting to frame the questioning and to obtain the necessary information. Because we are all human (even lawyers) he or she usually reviews the files from the initial briefing and finds they tend to have 5-10 additional questions and pieces of information they forgot to gather. That means reaching out again, and either asking via the phone or scheduling another meeting that takes up a full hour time slot even if it only takes an additional 30 minutes.

That means that the lawyer has now spent an extra hour, at least, gathering information for a particular case or filing. If that lawyer typically bills at even $200 an hour for their standard rate, and does this on an average with 5 clients per week, there is an additional $1,000 in revenue a week or $52,000 lost. This service revenue leak is more than likely not billable or is being billed unreasonably to clients who more than likely would be disgruntled if they knew they were being charged extra based on inefficiencies. Not to mention the time that it takes the lawyer to do these client tasks is time lost they can't be billing hours to current paying clients, assuming they are human and only work a certain number of hours per week.

This can also lead to poor reputation if savvy customers understand the process enough to know exactly what they are being charged for and start to talk about it to others in their circle of influence. It is also totally preventable through the minimal amount of time it would take to template out a general inquiry process that is required by clients to fill out prior to the appointment. This also allows the lawers to focus on building rapport during the meeting and having a better level of risk assessment of the case based on the conversation, rather than focusing on filling out information they need. And this is only one minor inefficiency in one process that law firm potentially has. The scariest part is that every single business has at least a handful of these unneccessary inefficiencies in every area of their business. Yikes!

Rule #5: Always Ask For And Use Customer Feedback.

Customer feedback and usage data is the only direct way to know the perspective and gaps created by your products and services. Though, there are other ways of guesstimating. While they could be very educated guesses, ultimately finding ways to get the brutal honesty that is in your customers mind is the best way to improve your business.

The only way to receive it, except for the very few proactive, raving-fan customers or the very angry opinionated customers, is to ask for it. Ask for it at every step up the process. Give incentives for giving feedback. Make giving feedback rewarding and safe for customers.

Also remember a key principle from the operations chapter, your employees are also your customers. And while in operations, customer feedback is used for the operations process, for products and services you are using that feedback to create or to better your products and service packages. Because, again, your employees also tend to be users of your product or service themselves and can offer key insights into better or more effective products and services.

Follow these five betterment rules for products and services, and you will ensure that the value you add will always add value back to your business for sustainable growth and longevity.

7. BETTERMENT LEADERSHIP

Leadership can seem a bit ubiquitous as you find yourself struggling to define the word and what exactly it means to your business. Leadership is one of those words that means different things to different people in different roles and positions within a company. In fact, in most businesses, people may even interchange the words manager and leader. And, in other cases, some even equate upper management with leadership qualities. Sometimes this is true and sometimes it isn't.

When it comes to the Business Betterment Mindset, leadership is a compilation of the strategic activities that navigate the direction of the organization *at every level*. It's key to understand that leadership at every level showcases the inclusiveness of the concept of leadership qualities.

Conversely, what we have historically seen as the definition of leadership under the growth mindset is the top-down decision making that *controls* the direction of a company. This type of leadership embraces the shareholder versus stakeholder mentality. It also limits who is involved in the overall decision making when it comes to the defined success of the organization and business. And, this type of leadership also does not promote conversation and trust, but rather promotes distrust and fear among team members. You see this happen because team members are not a part of the goal and strategy setting in any way. That lack of inclusiveness can imply a lack of trust to someone who wants to be active in the organization, which then results in fear of the unknown and lack of information and understanding about the organization. While it may seem foolish or difficult to have everyone in the organization involved, and to some who are concerned about "group think", not being at least more inclusive than your average company can have adverse effects on the sustainability of an organization dealing with high customer and team member turnover.

This isn't to say that every team member at every level needs to be involved and privy in every aspect of the business. It just means that giving leadership functionality and ownership or roles based on information that is beneficial to that specific position can have astounding effects on moral, longevity and commitment to the business.

Leadership, at every level, sets the tone for the culture of the organization. That's why it is so important for leadership to include every team member and leadership qualities to be cultivated in every team member.

In order to create that betterment in your business, leadership must be transparent from the head of the company through to every team member. Nothing should be so important that it can't be shared with every team member to the level that team members are a part of the overall business objectives, they understand them, and they believe in them. It is not enough to simply print out the set of objectives and hand them out. That is not the betterment model of leadership. Each member of the team must have a stake in the overall success of the organization to some extent beyond the inherent stake of a paycheck.

While you may feel there may be some circumstances that may require to be on a "need to know" basis, we would argue that the only areas that require complete discretion in most organizations are the areas of human resources and client security. Simply stated, personnel and client/customer files have to be maintained and kept private by whatever laws and policies govern your specific industry. Aside from this, the filter for which information gets shared isn't based on hierarchy, it's based on the ability for an individual in the company to understand the process behind decision making. If it can't be justified to every member of the team, given that a member has all necessary information and education to understand, then the action or business procedure probably isn't a justifiable action.

Beyond that, all planning, goals, objectives and budgets should be shareable among mostly everyone. How else would your internal team be able to take a role in leadership and thrive in their position as well as grow professionally? Your strategy becomes its finest version of execution in an open and transparent environment. And, as we stated before, this builds trust and ownership and accountability.

Leadership must be flexible and factor in, holistically, based on the culture of the business. Every aspect of your organization working together is what makes for a better business.

When leadership permeates every level of a business, the outcome becomes a very positive one because of that transparency and openness. Team members begin to engage with each other. There is a growing sense of self responsibility with commitment and loyalty to the values and visions of the business and organizations when you begin to see this transparency of leadership permeate the organization levels. A true sense of trust builds and fear or lack of trust dissipates among the team members who, up until this point, may not have felt valued or that their input and opinion mattered.

So, what are the important aspects of leadership? Starting by inspecting the concept of trust, all leadership requires courage and vulnerability. It takes courage to put your true authentic thoughts on the table and put aside the fear of judgement of current and past decisions that may not be "perfect." It takes being willing to fail and be seen as human and flawed as a member of the organization. It takes courage to allow others in to a conversation about a task or plan that ultimately is on your shoulders and that people could use pieces of that task or plan against you.

Leadership requires being a player in the game, not a bystander. And, this idea must happen from the CEO and owner down through every level of the business. When every team member is in the arena and willing to be there, they are engaged. And, to counter any arguments that team members, "just don't care", it is quite possible that the wrong team members are in place or true transparency is not present. Think about this idea as you read this chapter and beyond, especially the sections discussing culture, team and management.

Leadership decisions made with a betterment mindset are more likely to be met with the attraction of others in the business wanting to follow that same path of action. The right team members will be easier to recruit and retain in turn.

Imagine, as you read, seeing this leadership mindset move through your business. That's business betterment in ways that show strong team members actively engaged, promoting the business goals and creating growth in a redefined and sustainable way!

Below are the five rules that will ensure that betterment leadership is infused into your company.

Rule #1: Every Team Member Is A Leader.

Whether we want to believe it or not, we are always leading. This is true when we are at our best. This is also true if we are at our worst. That is because at its core leadership is a type of teaching and perception of our actions. It's a display of character and direction. And we as humans are always teaching and learning both consciously and subconsciously from those around us. When we connect with other people, we teach them what we believe through our perception and through our actions. We are observed and those observations lead to deductions that others choose to adopt, adapt to, or neither and walk away.

In essence, this is a core attribute of the "Transformational Leadership" theory. The best leaders help transform those around them to be the best version of themselves. A company full of individuals who are helping those around them (co-workers, vendors, customers, etc.) is a powerful company indeed.

Every individual of your company needs to know about leadership, what it means, and how they are personally responsible for it. With this information, anyone can develop strong, conscious leadership no matter what level of the company or career they are in. It may not be easy, but it can net your company outstanding employees. Employees that you helped polish from their former "diamond in the rough" state. This will require engagement, open conversation, truth through transparency and accountability.

While there are both natural and enforced hierarchies to leadership, personal and professional leadership at every level can be a secret weapon to productivity. It can also become employee ownership of their position and create people who think for the company, not just for themselves and how to coast through their 9-5 schedule.

Rule #2: Leadership Sets The Tone For Culture.

Leadership sets the tone for cultural awareness for reasons we've already stated including actions, transparency and trust. Based on this awareness, a culture emerges as a perception of what your team, customers, and community feel when they interact with your business.

Just a heads up. This isn't the only time culture will show up in our betterment rules. In fact, culture is its own chapter so you also have that to look forward to.

For our purposes in this section as culture relates to leadership, it is important to know that business betterment with an inclusive leadership style can have a profoundly positive impact on the culture of an organization.

Rule #3: Leadership Is Flexible And Factors Holistically.

Flexibility is the key word of a concept we have touched on a few times in this book already; adaptability.

Adaptability, or adaptive leadership states that the best leaders know how to adapt to the situations in which they find themselves and their companies in. Adaptive leadership takes letting go of expectations and being ready for whatever the next day, week, or year has in store. It's not so different in our personal lives. We look for solutions and opportunities and are poised to adapt, or we don't succeed because this is what life requires.

For the sake of clarity, we aren't saying your company shouldn't plan, have goals and hold expectations. However, even the best laid plans fall short of future realities because we are not omnipotent beings who have all of the variables at our disposal during the planning stages. What we do have is the ability, as long as we have the discipline and the ethical strength, to holistically plan.

Holistic planning is also a huge part of the stakeholder theory. Instead of only planning based on the wants and needs of shareholders (those who have a financial or power stake in the company) we plan with anything, anyone, and everyone who is affected by the decisions and actions of the company to the best of our ability to understand and predict. Again, while we can't plan for everything we can plan for as much as we have the capacity for at any given moment in time.

Some of the major stakeholders include your owners, shareholders, employees, customers, employee and customer families, vendors, joint venture partners, the communities your business operates in, the economy, the environment, other local businesses and nonprofits, as well as direct and indirect competitors. The input from these facets provides you and every leader with valuable data and insight that provides the necessary tools for agility in growth and betterment.

It is also helpful to establish an impact and "weight" to each stakeholder you either consider hypothetically or directly ask for input. This allows you to objectively look at how they are impacted by the business and decide how much they are affected. By their role as a stakeholder, you must also consider how much each affects your decision making based on their role in your company in the long term.

Establishing a weight and impact is an important part of knowing how much to take certain stakeholders into consideration. While a small vendor may be important in the decision making process, they most certainly aren't as impactful as your primary investors and customers. Therefore how it affects your primary investors and customers has a higher weight towards the decision that makes the most sense for positively serving them. But that doesn't mean that a small vendor of yours has zero weight or importance.

The more effort you put into this rule, the more factors you will have to make your decision and the more effortlessly you and your team will detect inconsistencies or conflicts in your actions that affect your major stakeholders and the business as a whole.

Rule #4: Strategy Is Collaborative At Its Finest.

Most companies see decision making as being a private, locked-boardroom process. While the final decision may be made in this vein on crucial decisions, almost every decision can be made better with more minds at play that are willing to offer constructive, confidential ideas.

The important thing to note for those who you choose to

involve but are not the final decision maker is for them to not get attached to their ideas or the outcome. Simply adding value to the conversation is a critical role, but holding on to an idea that doesn't get used can cause demotivation, so be explicitly clear about their role.

In a competitive environment, it makes sense that a lot of product and service talks can be threatened if exposed to competitors too early in development. More often than not, though, this risk threat is far less impactful than the brilliance and intellectual capacity gained by inviting other minds in the company, other than just high-level decision makers, into the product and service development decision making process.

An extreme but very well executed example of this is when coding and tech companies open-source their code to their communities and customers to help the company with complex lines of code or issues. This activity has led to huge technological advancements in these companies technologies and intellectual property that otherwise wouldn't have graced us at the consumer level in such a time frame. From the company's perspective, this was free labor that further invested their core customers in them as a company, creating raving fans, a community tribe and even a scouting opportunity for key talent that otherwise could cost millions to find or replicate.

Rule #5: Leadership Is Transparent.

Building on our last rule, in the perfect company, nothing is so important that it cannot be shared with your "lowest" of team members. The more your team member knows about the company, the more they are able to connect with the vision and become a part of it.

The biggest excuses we have seen in business for not being transparent are...

> *The company is doing something sub-par and doesn't want it leaking into the culture.*

This is akin to a child knowing they are doing something wrong but doing it anyway until someone of higher maturity enforces that it is wrong.

> *Intellectual property that has yet to be safe under copyright is in process.*

This is valid, but putting in the initial copyright on materials takes very little time and energy and expense and should not be an excuse for longer than a business week in hiding the processes from more and more team members who are trustworthy and credible employees.

> *The company is scared that their employees that aren't at a high-level will sell insider information to competitors or take that information and create a similar company or product.*

The only time this is usually an issue is with employees that are brand new, mistreated, or not very decent human beings. Therefore, be careful during probationary periods, treat your employees well, vet your hiring processes, and let go to reap the benefits of an open company. Typically in developement processes employees have to sign an agreement of confidentiality and non-compete or non-solicitation. These protect businesses from this situation and are simple to create. Don't let this stop you from building a better business.

If every cell in our body withheld its own information because it felt like its function was at jeopardy, our body could never work as a functional system, able to perform the actions required to live. And while our brain makes the final decision that leads to movement and action, it does so after receiving important sensory information from all areas of the body and its environment.

There you have it. Everything you need to deepen and better the leadership in your company.

Teach people to lead, lead people to teach. Set the correct tone of your company culture through your leadership principles and practices. Plan holistically but be flexible and adaptable to the outcome. Collaborate with anyone at any time possible that is willing to be constructive. Create transparency in the direction of your organization. Rinse. Repeat. Reap the benefits.

8. BETTERMENT MANAGEMENT

Management

We've decided to separate out the topics of leadership and management. It wasn't really even a conversation or a close call. It's non-negotiable in our betterment model. While management involves leadership, very distinct differences do exist. And, within the betterment mindset, the distinct differences within these areas are key to creating business betterment. Hopefully after reading this chapter, everyone will understand why leadership and management are clearly two independent concepts.

As defined from a business betterment perspective, management is the inclusive oversight of resources and activities that are executed in an effort to further a business' objectives as opposed to a top-down decision making that controls the direction of the company.

What's the difference? The business betterment model

suggests that a dictatorship-like model simply doesn't work when it comes to sustainable growth. The people executing the activities to achieve business success are one of the most important assets a company has in order to achieve success. Why wouldn't you ensure that management was inclusive? And the other piece of that "dictatorial" approach is that it doesn't simply not promote inclusiveness but rather specifically promotes exclusiveness. If the manager becomes the "keeper" of information or power exclusively, he or she risks alienating the team which can create an atmosphere of distrust, discontent, and even withholding important insights and information from that manager.

Management holds the keys to insights and operative betterment when it comes to understanding that objectives are expectations and not always reality. Management is often the liaison from operations directly to their teams. And what that looks like, especially in a larger organization, is an open line between managers and the team on such key issues as operational impact on products and services. This definitely includes important business operations such as budgets, development and distribution. When the lines of communication are open, teams work better together as they better understand the goals and, even more importantly, expectations.

Managers are the best conduits for communication within any organization, keeping lines open between departments and among upper management.

While in a business practicing the business betterment

movement, a larger organization will still have a staffing and resource structure for efficiency. This really makes management a key component to overall effectiveness and sustainable growth and isn't necessarily promoting a "flat" company hierarchy.

As with leadership, management practices must be built on trust. In order to create that efficiency that is so necessary for a betterment business, transparency is essential. With that transparency, trust becomes a by-product that creates a higher level of efficiency and effectiveness among the team members.

In a manager's role, there is more involved than just decision making and resource oversight. Direct managers are the front-line of building loyalty, excitement and self responsibility in employees in order to create sustainable growth from all team members.

A manager is a valuable resource that can rally the troops, create momentum and build loyalty that produces the best products and services possible for customers. In this way, you could say that managers are a specific or sub-type of leader, and these betterment rules are five sub-rules for leaders who happen to also be managers.

Rule #1: People Are More Important Than Objectives.

It is really easy as a manager to get caught up in the day-to-day of responsibilities that are very task-oriented and time consuming. This can take away from the time spent building team motivation and excitement. These responsibilities usually include measurements and metrics to fulfill to ensure overall company and business strategic objectives continue to be met. Objectives set a precedent, but in and of themselves they mean nothing without team members to fulfill them. In other words, your objectives are only as important as your people are productive. And, news flash, people aren't productive for long if they aren't valued. Again we go back to that point of inclusiveness and its overall importance to the business. When team members feel valued and included, they work harder, are more loyal and hold themselves to a very different level of accountability and ownership of the results of their role in reaching the business objectives.

Tasks and to-dos are based off of leadership planning, but so is culture and betterment, managers understand this. What this means is that, while the day-to-day work must get done in order to meet the necessary objectives, sustainable success will come from creating that business betterment mindset and putting it into action.

Consensus: Managers of all levels should be focused on their people first, and their objectives second. In fact, maybe their employees should be their objectives? When managers focus on their people, the people then feel empowered and valued and the end result is those day-to-day activities get done with haste, enthusiasm and accountability.

Rule #2: Dictatorship Doesn't Work.

As we begin building off of rule number one in tandem with something we discussed in the leadership chapter, holding and abusing power without any form of collaboration can dismantle a department and at times even a country if you take that broad brush against this idea from a global, historical and a deep personal observation standpoint.

Taking the lead, using your position of power and being firm are tools in a toolkit that may have to be used in certain situations, but as a rule there are usually better ways and better tools that can be used with employees which managers are responsible for.

Talking *at* and not *with* your team can be the difference in the total direction of a managers department or area of the company.

Employees will not forget who has final say and who is the decision maker as a manager, reminding them and flaunting authority is a misuse of power that happens all too often. And, to reiterate, this kind of behavior in a business breeds distrust and will ultimately have an impact on the quality of the products and services delivered as well as relationships with customers.

Rule #3: Management Holds Answers To Operative Betterment.

Looking from the top down as the CEO or COO, you

should know that managers at all levels can have crucial insights into how things can be run better from an operational and a customer service standpoint. Especially if they follow many of the betterment principles outlined in this book.

A good manager is someone employees come to for support, for internal complaints about processes, procedures, customer complaints and of course the "wins" from customer service delivered. They also observe many situations that most people in the organization don't have the time, energy or stamina for because they are often on the front lines with customers, products or customer support and distribution.

These insights can lead to profound benefits, if they are utilized correctly within a company. If you are at the top of the company chain, find ways to engage your managers from an informational perspective that heavily includes interaction and dialogue. Learn how to catalog this information and use it for planning and betterment cycles.

If you are an employee or floor level manager and supervisor, find ways to catalog your informational observations and input from employees and find ways to communicate it to upper level management without compromising the integrity of your employee relationships and confidentiality. This will not only benefit the company, should they choose to use it, but your organizational skills can and often will lead to individual gain and benefits.

Rule #4: Operations Are Expectations, Not Reality.

Dang. You caught us. This rule is very, very similar to rule #3 in the leadership chapter. Like we said, leadership and management have many similarities and this is one major overlap that we felt needed a second pass.

Yes. Set expectations. Strive for them. But do not dwell on them. Expectations are fluid and can change as conditions in the work environment, market environment and community environment change. It is important to set expectations that are flexible, as change happens around you and your business and as you recognize this change from manager and employee input.

Dwelling on expectations will always lead to an abuse of rule #1. If an objective is missed or not accomplished it can lead to organizational pressure. If a manager holds this pressure personally, it usually gets vented and purged to employees, which creates a negative internal reaction to the situation or objective. This can decrease productivity and more importantly decrease loyalty and connection to the manager and therefore to the company. This can lead to human resource expenses for the uncreative response of the irritable manager responsible for a quota. A quota which was made via a subjective, educated guess or from productivity based on the past. Working with your employees and teams through dialogue about those changing environments allows you to better understand and revise expectations realistically, thus still inevitably meeting business objectives.

Don't fall into this organizational disaster circle. Avoid it by letting go of the past, considering the results and current reality of the opportunity cost and look to the future instead.

Rule #5: Managers Are Conduits.

Managers are supposed to have information and be *excited* to share it. This also follows the betterment rule of transparency. Without the proper information, there isn't a proper energetic flow of betterment from the top of the company down to the line employee.

If your company can acknowledge that managers are conduits, enforcers and encouragers of information, then processes and procedures can be put into place to allow managers to do what they are best at and that is to be leaders to their team with the fullest possible potential.

These five rules produce outstanding managers. Outstanding Managers that work *for* the company and are about sustainable production because their principles and practices are sustainable.

Abusing one or more of these rules will result in poor employee morale, an increase expenses of hiring and rehiring for the same positions, and finding that only "C" and "D" level performers are staying around long enough to fully grasp or perform their positions.

Use managers for answers to company challenges. Don't

allow managers to abuse their power at the detriment to employees. Give managers all necessary information. Allow them to be flexible with parameters. And give managers the opportunity and training to focus on their team members above all else.

9. BETTERMENT TEAMS

A very large part of creating betterment in your business is truly recognizing and understanding who makes up your team in its most simplistic form. It is your team that works to drive your business purpose and passion through their support and involvement of the business goals and objectives.

For the purposes of the business betterment mindset, your team consists of all of the people who support the fulfillment of your products and services. The key to this idea is to consider the word ALL when you think about who supports the fulfillment of your offerings which could also include mentors, life coaches, teachers and trainers.

In an isolated growth-only focused world and mindset, your team is defined as the human resources used to further your company's bottom line. The focus excludes those who aren't on payroll and is often narrowly defined by job roles as opposed to meaningful contribution. Most in this type of team have defined roles and are not encouraged to reach and grow outside that box.

What's the difference here? The business betterment mindset is inclusive as we've mentioned before in this book in other organizational aspects. It doesn't simply look at your team as monetary assets, but rather looks at your team as those people who nurture growth.

By joining the Business Betterment Movement, you will be fostering relationships *on purpose* with people who build meaningful experiences in the office and for the customer.

Your team, as a part of business betterment model, includes your staff, your vendors, your customers, your community, your friends and your family. Basically, your team is anyone and everyone that you rely on to reach the idea of success in business even if they are a part of your personal life. Furthermore, the success you then experience is a reflection on anyone that supports your efforts, both personally and professionally.

Think about this: we all need a sounding board for ideas, challenges, and even frustrations. Those sounding boards are likely not your paid staff all the time. They may be your family, friends, business colleagues, coaches, or whoever else you choose to be your outlet. And, these team members are as vital to your overall success as your staff, vendors and customers in the long term. They keep us sane in the hardest of times in our business.

Your community and your involvement in your community is also vital to your success. While many of these people and organizations may not be customers, they are supporting you in the community and helping you be a better person which is also reflected in your business activities. Especially when it comes to the public opinion and perception of your business. Your community can be one of the best support systems for utilizing your products and services and talking about them! While you may not be charging for all of your time as is the case with volunteer work and community outreach, the benefits can still be measurable and offer substantial long-term return. If you work on your community, your community will want to work with you!

It is easy to say, "volunteer organizations only want to work with me because my time is free. When it comes down to it, they won't want to pay for my products or services" This mindset can lead to not putting in the effort to connect with your community because there is so much other billable and back office work that needs to be done. And while it may be true for some that when it comes down to paying for products or services they just won't, no matter how much time you put into community involvement with them. But there are also always people who will. On the other hand, if there is no connection or involvement made, there is no amount of "free" that is beneficial to anyone or any opportunity to find those community members who will engage in your business.

Altruism really only works when it is mutually beneficial. You must as a business feel you are truly making a difference, which gives you and your team a sense of accomplishment wether it's volunteer work, creating community events or going to networking opportunities. And your community must feel the benefit of your sincerity and commitment. Then, at some point, you will realize you are experiencing a community team that is supporting your business with business.

Now, turning to your internal team, the methods for finding the right people in order to thrive is an important intellectual property. Once you have found that magic formula for finding the right people for your team and organization, document it, use it and reap the benefits. And by following the betterment mindset, you will find that success in recruiting and retaining your team is much easier than with exclusively following a growth mindset.

Finding your team really is an art form. When it comes to identifying your internal team, it is important to choose those people who share your values and visions. The foundation must be built on trust as with any of your relationships in business and in life.

Encourage all of your team to provide you with feedback and do so with safety. Your team should feel confident that they will not experience backlash for respectfully candid feedback. Ask your vendors how it is to do business with you. Is it a good experience? Why or why not? Does your internal team feel comfortable in sharing ideas and providing feedback on how processes work within the scope of their job description? They should.

Instead of taking the attitude of "I'm paying you so just

do what I say," adopt the attitude of learning and collaboration. Encourage conversation among everyone.

This attitude of "just do it" doesn't address the motivations that will ultimately save you money spent on a team, which is one of the highest expenditures, that is driven by fear instead of by excitement of contribution and success.

As we will discuss in the chapter on Culture, this attitude also breeds a culture of fear and distrust. If your team feels that you view them solely as an expendable resource a certain distrust will grow which really does impede success and commitment.

Your external team of supporters, including friends, must be built on that same foundation of trust. Your life and your business does not have room for toxicity or negativity that does not match your values. Transparency and authenticity are absolutely key elements of your overall team and those who support you in fulfilling business.

Rule #1: Companies Growing Individuals Grow Individuals Who Grow Companies.

This is a powerful statement. More than that, we would argue that if we had to pick one, this would be the most important rule for betterment in a company. Period. How about we break it down.

Companies growing individuals. This means that a company is invested in the betterment of each individual of their company. They have adopted a betterment mindset and are invested in their people in such a way that people get behind the company, believe in its vision and have a sense of loyalty and unencumbered commitment. All because they simply feel valued.

Grows Individuals. By focusing on the betterment of individuals, those team members become better, more educated, more advanced in their human-oriented and task-oriented skills. They also individually recognize their own growth which translates to commitment to achieving more for themselves and the business.

Who Grow Companies. These individuals invest their new found skills into the companies they are working for. The more each individual grows, the more the company they work for grows and becomes better through them.

This is the essence of growth by focusing on betterment. This is what can result when you focus on and support the people on your team.

Rule #2: Your Methods Of Finding And Hiring The Right People Is An Important Intellectual Property.

In fact, it is one of the most important processes your company can catalog outside of products and services intellectual property. So many businesses fail early because they are a one-man-band with an amazing idea and no idea how to find the right people to foster that vision into a solid existence. Don't let that be your company.

As you read this book, you will begin to understand and adopt the betterment mindset and how it can impact your hiring process. When you understand the impact of inclusiveness, you will see incredible results in the people you attract and retain.

Once you've adopted the betterment mindset, you can create systems and a repeatable process for finding and hiring the right people. This process will become more and more efficient and effective over time.

Rule #3: Independent Contractors, Joint Venture Relationships And Vendors Are Team Members.

Many businesses we work and consult with consider the companies they also work with to fulfill production needs a necessary part of doing business. They offer services and products that the company needs to provide their own products and services effectively, which can range from printing and design to consulting and human resource help. These companies are more than what they offer as vendors, they are a part of your team.

A company's contractors, joint ventures and vendors are crucial team members that should be entered into relationships with in the same vane as you would hire a new employee. Rule #1 isn't just talking about your location and hiring processes for internal employees. The better your vetting processes for external team members, the stronger and more rewarding these relationships will be from a loyalty, service and potentially even financial standpoint.

Rule #4: "Team" Includes Personal And Non-Operative Support Networks.

You and your employees each have a network of their own connected and also detached from the company. These networks provide us individual support. They help us get through tough times, give us rides to the airport, offer business tips and advice, mentor us, etc.

This is actually a strength to the company because the larger each individual team members personal network, the more stable that employee is and potentially more people that individual can reach as a potential consumer of your company's products and services.

Treating these networks as indirect resources by acknowledging and understanding each team member's individual networks to the best of our ability can have a strong impact on widening the company's sphere of influence and deepening its roots in any community.

Rule #5: Effective Team Resource Usage = Efficient Spending.

This includes all of the team members we listed above. Employees, independent contractors, joint ventures, vendors, support and other networks.

The more effectively and consistently you better the relationships with each team member, the more value you are getting out of your team member expenses.

For each dollar you spend on a relationship, there is an efficiency return. Sometimes your people use their time and skills more efficiently for that dollar, sometimes they waste it. The better educated, equipt, trained, informed, and motivated they are, the more efficiently they are using each dollar you spend on them. Obviously this applies the most to employees, but also applies to all other team members to some extent.

Your team is a company resource. That is why they are called human resources. The more effectively you use your team resources, the better you motivate your internal and external team, ultimately the more effectively you are utilizing the internal payroll and independant contractor cost of your business.

Following and using these five betterment rules will help you build a stronger, more valuable team.

Focus on the betterment of each individual. Get better and better at finding and hiring the right people. Change your perspective of vendor, independent contractor and joint venture relationships. Learn how to access and support the networks of each team member.

Do this more effectively over time and one of your largest expenses will pay itself back ten fold for your organization.

10. BETTERMENT CULTURE

Another very large part of creating betterment in your business is recognizing and having an understanding of what your company culture is in its most raw form. It is also understanding the meaning of the word "culture" in the first place. For our purposes, and we'll continue this discussion further in the chapter, we define the word culture to mean, "That feeling you get when you have an experience with a company."

Our definition of culture is that feeling and perception that is created when any team member or stakeholder or *potential* stakeholder is thinking about their experience with your business. It's the culmination of how the world views your company. It's a spreading of ideals through actions.

It is easy to casually say things like, "we have a culture of kindness," or "we have a culture of nurturing, growth and advancement." But what do these statements really mean to you and each and every person on your team? How true are they to the people and supporters who really matter?

It's important to be candid with ourselves and with each other on any team in terms of talking openly about culture. Are the cultural statements that are being spoken taken out of a leadership book because they sound great? Are they what you *hope* your business is or want to become? Or are they a culmination of clear observations and direct feedback about what comes to mind when people think of your business?

Having that candid discussion in a safe environment will bring to light the reality of what the true culture is in your business. It is an important conversation that needs to take place. A good way to start is to create a survey for your team, vendors, and customers that allows for initial confidentiality and asks questions about experiences with the business.

There are no wrong answers here. The important and very key answer is the one that speaks to the absolute truth which means it is essential to provide a safe environment for their answers.

The best cultures are ones where your employees, customers and the outside world believe four things. One, that you provide phenomenal products and services. Two, you care about your employees. Three, you care about your customers. And four, you care about the world.

If all of the people who think of your company believe these four things, then your culture perpetuates positivity and value back to your company.

Under the "growth only through spreadsheet" definition of culture, it is defined by the company as, "the logic used to mold team members to a specific mindset and way of being." It is set from the top as a way a company wants to be perceived or is pretending to be, not necessarily the reality of peoples perception.

And, not understanding the true "culture" of your business, or by defining it in a vacuum, you can end up setting the stage for fear. This could include fear of retaliation, fear of providing authentic input and fear of losing a job if people don't believe or distrust this seemingly dictated way to think. In fact, this approach can have an adverse effect on your overall business preventing sustainable growth in employees, sales and customer retention. This is seen through customer service not being at its finest and sales being dictated only by dollars because of lack of belief and trust in the business which ultimately impacts the bottom line of a company.

It's important to also embrace the idea that culture is not and cannot be established by one single person and should never be used as a tool to control your team.

Culture is one of the single biggest components to creating the trust every company tries to build within your community, organization and team.

By understanding the true culture of your business, you will be creating a new loyalty base from your team members, customers and community, a new transparency and a new way of communicating that promotes and generates a higher quality of relationships. And the very cool thing about all of this is that it can go a long way to driving efficiency, personal happiness and company happiness which all transcends to the customer and their individual experience.

As you're contemplating this idea of culture, you may find that, through some soul searching, you aren't exactly sure if we're on the same page when it comes to business betterment. What we mean by this statement is that some businesses may feel or believe they follow the betterment model, especially as it relates to the culture of the business, but recognize after having these candid conversations that there are discrepancies between actual experience and perceived experience.

Here's our answer to that; sometimes a company's actions have a lag in cultural perception. A company cannot simply decide to do or be something new, and except that trust is immediately earned. If you and your decision making management team truly believe you are on the path to a betterment culture after the five betterment rules below, you probably are. But your customers and team members need time to experience and process that before it becomes an ingrained perception.

The culture of your business must be based on the betterment of the business. What do we mean by that? Culture is an ideal that is based on shared values. It is not a tool to control subordinates or other team members or force them into a value system that doesn't fit with their own. Culture, based on shared values has authenticity and integrity and is the single biggest factor in retention, loyalty and happiness inside and outside of your organization.

In an organization that has joined this business betterment movement, you will see very clear indications of a "we're in this together" mentality based on acceptance of opinions that are grounded in positive change and complete equality. You won't see a management versus team members mentality in a culture that's rooted in the business betterment movement.

And, in this culture, you find that it becomes easier to hire new team members because you have a very clear idea of what type of person with a specific value system will fit into your overall organizational structure. You will also see sales and customer retention becomes easier because your true values will be transparent which means attracting the right customers.

The key to creating business betterment is to have a culture that literally incubates the qualities of humanity that grows with pride as the business grows and changes.

This approach takes a certain mindfulness and clarity, not to mention a completely open awareness of the strengths and weaknesses of each and every person within the organization. It's a meaningful experience that creates and defines purpose for the entire company.

Every one of us needs to feel purpose, to have a purpose, and be able to act on that purpose. With the right mindset within a business, you will work with your team members and their strengths and weaknesses to find the perfect fit for the purpose of the business and personal values. And this becomes your business' culture.

The question then becomes, how do you get there? How do you achieve that foundation of business betterment that we find in our organization's culture?

Read on.

Creating an environment that fosters transparency and acceptance of differing suggestions and opinions means creating an environment that encourages open and positive communication. And this means all team members including controllers, sales teams, literally everyone right up to the owner, being as open to hearing others perceptions as they are willing to discuss and share *their* perceptions and wants in the businesses culture.

A good exercise is to take some time with your team, out of the office if it can be arranged, and create an environment to openly discuss shared values, purpose and change. This is a great follow-up to a preliminary survey that gets team members minds warmed up and ready for the idea of a conversation around culture.

These three ideas of values, purpose and change, can take shape in a number of ways and in a number of different categories.

For example, you will want to address values as it pertains to the values of your brand, your services and your own personal life. You may find that your own personal values match those of your services, products and brand. Especially if you are an owner/operator. These three don't *need* to be the exact same, but they *cannot* contradict eachother. It is important for this to hold true with each and every one of your team members. Their personal values cannot contradict the values (or their preceived values) of the brand, products or services that they interact with in your organization.

Open up the discussion with the basic question of defining a personal set of values. Authenticity? Compassion? Boldness? And, to each person, what do these values look like? Have each person create a description that is meaningful to him or her and even include an example to get the team started based on your definition.

As you go through this exercise you will begin to establish the shared values of your team members and begin to relate them to the values of your business. The conversations will also lead you into the identification of the strengths of the individuals and the entire group as a whole.

Rule #1: Culture Must Be Based On The Betterment Of Business And The Individuals Within.

When your culture is based around bettering your product or service and the way you distribute it, it becomes a collaborative effort to do better. This creates an environment of motivation for quality.

When your culture is based around bettering those

within it, you create a culture where everyone matters. If basic survival needs are met, almost nothing is stronger than the human need to belong and be acknowledged. Everyone wants to contribute. When we as humans feel like we are not contributing or living up to their potential in a company it lowers our self-esteem and production.

By focusing on betterment, it allows your company to build a culture easily and without complex plans or control measures and one that is based on authenticity and transparency.

Rule #2: Culture Is The Spreading Of Ideas.

What else would it be? Culture isn't a tangible, visible thing. Unless you are talking about kombucha or something else you can touch or taste. Culture is a culmination of shared ideas about what the company considers important in its values. One single person doesn't establish what culture is. There will always be those who have a different perspective of your company from the norm, but in general there is a consensus about your company based primarily around your company's actions.

For instance, when REI exclaimed to the world that it wasn't going to be open on Black Friday and instead encouraged people to get outside and be with friends and family, they in that moment further ingrained that their culture is about adventure and connection. If they had simply said "go outside, but also come to our store for deals," there would be virtually no impact on their brand or internal culture. Actions create widespread opinions and perspectives about your company, and the spreading of these ideals creates your culture.

The important takeaway from this example is in the word "actions." Think of it as an update to the old saying, "actions speak louder than words." What we are saying is , "you words must be followed by action, or they mean very little." What you do must fall right in line with what you say. That is the perception and your perceived culture.

Rule #3: Culture Is Not A Tool To Control Subordinates.

Culture should never be a control device to use over your team. It isn't a way to manipulate those in your company to do what you want as a way of forcing them to feel better within your company. Culture, ultimately, should be for the sake of culture and not a means to an end. When culture is determined by what it *should* be instead of what it *is*, it lacks true feeling and is not authentic and therefore not sustainable. Remember in previous chapters we discussed that this lack of authenticity can actually create an environment of fear and distrust instead of loyalty and commitment.

Ironically, thinking of culture as a means to achieve something else is ultimately counterproductive to building the culture itself, because once that something is achieved the emphasis on company culture begins to deteriorate until those with decision making power find another use for it as a way to further their gain. This is not the purpose of a well-defined culture. In other words, if a business is using a forced culture to achieve something that is not in line with the true values of a company, it will ultimately become detrimental to the company. It always comes back to that "walk the talk" mentality.

Rule #4: Culture Is The Single Biggest Factor In Retention, Loyalty And Happiness. Inside And Out Of The Organization.

What your company represents and how your company is viewed creates a reason for team members and customers to stay. Culture becomes the reason they rave about you and at a fundamental level how much fulfillment your employees feel in life and in their passions. If a large portion of an employee's life is spent working for your company, then your company is shaping their life, wellness and fulfillment. The more positive, uplifting, encouraging, passionate, compassionate, open and transparent your company culture is the more an employee will be able to thrive and the more customers will see the benefit of supporting it.

A business could argue that it is there products and services that give people a reason to stay. However the experience from research and development, through production, through fulfillment is all affected by culture and the experience people have, and that shows in the final product. Culture can have a huge impact on the retention of those on both sides of the product life cycle if you let it and cultivate it to thrive.

Rule #5: A Better Culture Is One That Continually Incubates The Qualities Of Humanity That Future Generations Would Be Proud To Associate And Follow.

A truly authentic culture based on the reality of experience and connection to actual values bolsters a company and helps to build a reputation packed with integrity and an obvious commitment to quality, community and people.

How do you do this? With these simple questions: how do we leave the world better than we found it? Today? This week? This month? This quarter? This year? How do we do that within the company? How do we do that outside of the company?

Be honest, be real. Address the challenges and walk the talk. Your culture will be one with your values. People will notice. People will talk about it and people will want to engage more and more in your company.

Before we wrap up the chapter, we want to offer a word of warning on change, negativity and how it relates to a cultural spiral.

Change is inevitable, and if your company is a cultivator of positive change in culture, operations, marketing, sales, leadership, and beyond then the company you have built will never die easily. Equally, along the way if your company does not embrace positive change and cultivate it, individuals and groups within your company will experience intentional inequalities, hate, and inhumanity. Whether it was intentional or not, If this happens within your company, it needs to be addressed. Immediately. Toxicity breeds and replicates like aggressive cancer within your company culture and a single person can darken the culture of an entire department if not recognized and dealt with promptly.

Betterment teams involve fostering meaningful experience with purpose. Not tailgating on ideas about poor intentions or the company and working conditions. There are always going to be people who sit in a dark cloud and try to bring others into their rainy day parade. Take a stance about how your business feels about this and in what ways this is against the grain of what you are building. Then, let your actions speak for themselves.

Playing off of rule number four and taking it a bit deeper, fostering that meaningful experience cultivates and grows a customer loyalty based on honesty and integrity. Your internal team thrives with having a purpose, resulting in higher commitment to quality, open communication and personal accountability.

And, culture plays a large role, not only in the leadership and management of your business, but also in your branding and overall marketing. That culture comes through in all aspects of marketing, which we will discuss in the next chapter. Make your culture tangible and sustainable and based on action commitments. watch it flourish and build your organization through your marketing efforts.

11. BETTERMENT MARKETING

Marketing is a huge concept that a lot of smaller businesses just simply avoid altogether. Hopefully, from a foundational perspective, this chapter will help clarify what marketing is and how to approach it for betterment. Marketing has been Jennifer's specialty and an area of passion, as she loves to see businesses tell their authentic stories and thrive through those stories. If you feel your company could be doing marketing better, we are here to light the spark!

First things first. What constitutes marketing and marketing activities? Marketing is a big world and incorporates the activities pertaining to brand strategy, strategic planning, messaging, content creation, storytelling, advertising, social media, collateral, logos, and reputation management. Marketing is anything that involves building awareness for your company and brand.

The impact of such activities, especially when they are done with the betterment mindset, will become evident in the increased awareness of your business. This translates to increased sales over time because more people will know and be interested in your products and services. A secondary, but equally important, impact is the pride and camaraderie that builds on your team when marketing is done right.

And, the difference between sales and marketing (we'll talk about sales in the next chapter) is that marketing will set the tone for sales to happen. Marketing happens in front of and around sales.

When you decide to join the betterment movement for your business, the world and your options within it change in general. This includes the world of marketing.

In a world of business betterment, marketing uses the brand and personality of the business for creating awareness of who you are and what you do. Most importantly, it sets the stage for creating a conversation with customers, with your team, with the community and even with yourself.

In the growth-only world of marketing, and the current gold-standard accepted approach of just making the most noise anywhere possible to be heard, we see ourselves as setting the stage for sales and nothing more. Marketing messages and activities are dictated by sales instead of being inclusive. In other words, we create the lure. We create the hook that will start a conversation with a potential customer or client for the sales process to begin. We view marketing as the medium to talk to the world in order to *convince* or plant the seed that a person or group needs a particular product or service. What makes this different than the betterment mindset approach is the word "convinced."

If you find yourself having to actively convince customers to "like" you and buy from you, it is time to revisit the core of your business. Go back and review the questions in previous chapters to get you started or back on the right path.

And, a reality with marketing is that it is an expense line item and not one that generally directly creates revenue. We attribute the revenue generating to sales. And it is because of this reality that oftentimes, marketing doesn't get the full attention or even resources that it deserves and needs to create those incredible conversations which we see often in a growth-only mindset.

There is a difference in the priorities of shareholders, operations teams and the marketing team. It's about budget and time versus pressure versus high quality versus authentic marketing. The betterment rules for marketing bring all of these areas together so that all priorities are met with as few compromises as possible from each invested party.

It's time to show that marketing has value way beyond a number in the expense column. When you adopt this idea of business betterment wholly, you will find that you focus less on what it's costing you and instead on what it's gaining you.

Your brand, your message and your identity is how the world sees you, for better or for worse. This idea is the betterment mindset of inclusiveness. The activities within your marketing efforts are based on the transparency of internal conversations as well as external communications with your community and customers. If those conversations are not authentic, your team and customers will eventually discover it and it can be detrimental to your business.

That hook, and lure or that "convincing" that is not authentic, has the sole purpose of reeling in the customer for the sales rep, whomever on your team is managing that particular process.

Oftentimes we find ourselves in purely growth-by-numbers mode, focusing on what we believe the customer should be listening to when it comes to our products. Even worse is when we convey to our prospective customers what we believe they want to hear versus what we are actually offering. Sometimes, what a prospective customer wants to hear may not be what we can deliver to them in the way of solutions of products that meet their needs. It is extremely important to be honest and keep exaggerations at bay. Even if we have a deep desire to fill an unfillable need, trying to do so and not meeting that need is always going to be the worst case scenario in terms of reputation and customer retention.

When you accept and adopt a betterment approach, you are accepting a willingness to listen to your customers with an open mind, sincerity and transparency. Then, your message and what you convey and promise to your customers is truthfully how you want the world to see you.

We discuss in this book the importance of transparency internally with your team. This transparency ensures that you are conducting your business with betterment in mind. We also urge you to create your products and motivate your team in the right manner and with the right intentions.

Working with your customers should be done in very much the same way. It does require looking in the mirror at yourself and your business as you would when deciding to adopt the betterment mindset. Are you willing to engage in a conversation with customers knowing that you may not entirely like everything that is discussed? Are you willing to accept that, perhaps what you've been telling them you provide may not entirely be accurate and set the course straight?

We're not suggesting that dishonesty is taking place within your business. But, every road is always paved with the best intentions. We want to make our customers happy. We want to do everything we can for them. Sometimes promises with good intentions are made in the hopes of impressing our customers to keep them. This approach almost always backfires.

Marketing in the world of business betterment means not tricking customers into buying. It means having a transparent dialogue whereby all parties know what to expect, creating a sense of loyalty and credibility and connection based on what is important.

The question is, where do you start? Well, the best way to start is to tell your own story, the good, the bad and the ugly.

This is your opportunity to tell your story, connect with your audience, and make someone's life better because of what you have to offer that person that meets a challenge or solves a problem.

Your story consists of all of the why's, the what's, the who's, the where's, the when's and the how's of where your business was, where it is and where it's going. Why did you choose the business that you're in today? What happened or changed in your life that prompted you to go down this road? When did you make this decision to go into this business or create this product that you are offering today? How did you get started? Who inspired you? Who helped you? Where were you when you decided this was the business for you? Where did you decide to anchor your business and why? What were some of the challenges you had to overcome? What were some of the successes?

These are just a few of the questions that, when answered, provide a solid, inspiring and motivating story for just the right audience. And, it's that audience that will relate to your story in your marketing and become team members and customers.

Your story is what helps you build your brand personality and brand identity in a very authentic way. Marketing in the world of business betterment is always truthful and transparent. And, believe it when we say it, and we've said it before, lies *always* come to the surface.

some may find themselves challenging this statement and even getting a bit defensive. However, even one seemingly small indiscretion about your product or service will defeat your efforts to build loyalty and will create distrust among your team and your customers.

Take software companies, or even more specifically those who fund game developers. Many have had the mindset of producing as many games as possible as fast as possible. The result is an extremely large array of games on the market for customers to choose from. The impact is now a much more discriminating customer because they can sit with all of the choices available. And, those developers rushing to the market may not have stellar or even finished products. The best game developers, and those that have won countless awards, are the ones who put quality over quantity. They make claims and uphold them. If they have a beta product, they say it is a beta product. They don't sell a beta product as a full priced product.

One of the first questions we often ask our own clients is "who is your ideal customer?" More often than not, we're met with the response of "anyone who will buy my product." But is that really true? Aren't you, rather, providing solutions to the customers that need your solution to make their lives better? These are the customers you connect with in the deepest way. And that's not "anyone that will buy your product or service." It is virtually impossible to service everyone as not everyone needs what you have to offer or doesn't relate to your "why."

Your product or service is one that should be providing a

positive impact in someone's life. That's the transparency in your marketing message. Marketing and creating awareness is, at its best, about creating a better world through using your product or service.

As you construct your story, you'll discover key words and descriptions that will then begin to organically formulate the words of your message. When transparency and authenticity are used in creating your marketing message, it's incredible how easy it can become. Why is that? Because it's who *you* are! it naturally flows from a place of ease because you understand and are aligned with the reason you are providing the product or service.

As you dialogue with your customers, some of the key questions you can be asking them are, "why did you choose my product?" and "how did this product make your life better?" The answers to those questions can be very telling indeed and can also create the fodder you need to continue to build your marketing communications plan, brand identity and strategy as well as all of the advertising and collateral you will need.

And so the connection to your customer base begins, paving the way for sales and growth but from a place of credibility, loyalty and transparency.

Rule #1: The Purpose Of Marketing Is To Build Awareness Of And Interest In A Product Or Service.

This is the only purpose. This is more of a definition but it is an important one to remember. The question in terms of marketing is either:

"How do we build awareness that we or a particular offering exists?" or ,

 "How do we build interest in a product that a customer already knows exists?"

These two questions begin every marketing process of a betterment model. The answers should always convey and exemplify your company's true values, passions and positive actions.

Rule #2: Marketing, At Its Best, Is About Bettering The World.

The best and most impactful marketing efforts can change the world. Either a little or a lot. It can create positive trends. It can uplift a community. It can make someone smile. It can give someone hope. And the best part of all of these efforts is that they are based on the truth and transparency that your customers notice and your team identifies with.

If marketing is approached first by what it's looking to achieve for a product or service, followed closely by how it can positively impact those who come into contact with it, something is going right. Remember we said your product or service should make a difference? This translates to marketing that makes a difference, especially when you connect on a very personal level with your prospective community.

Rule #3: Marketing Lays The Foundation For Building Relationships.

Marketing lays the foundation of building relationships which is the foundation for sales to occur. Therefore marketing tends to effortlessly float into sales. Because of this it can be really difficult to tell the difference between where marketing ends and sales begins. It can also be difficult to know how to lead a customer from one to the other.

That is why it is key to understand what foundational efforts marketing is making for the relationships your company is building in its customers and community.

Additionally, it is important to find and define where and how sales begins through marketing based on the different ways customers can approach your company.

This is accomplished through the upfront efforts of aligning marketing efforts and objectives with those of the sales efforts. Remember, this cannot be done in a vacuum. It must be done with the inclusiveness of operations, management and feedback from customers. This alignment will help you define those specific areas where your marketing efforts and sales efforts are in the relationship-building phase. Then you can easily track the closure rate of sales.

You can accomplish this intangible divide by working in communication efforts that provide information on how the customer found you in the first place.

If this is done right, marketing can be more justified by showing how it drives sales and either creates leads or makes them more "warm" in the sales process.

Rule #4: Marketing Has Value Beyond The Expense It Shows.

Speaking of justifying marketing budgets, it's important to know that marketing is more than just the expense it shows on paper.

Many times marketing gets cut first in a product or department or even the company as a whole. Which, by the way is usually the sign of some dysfunction in a department, product or the organization and marketing is simply the symptom, not the cause of the issue. Think about this, what cause is a company attempting to treat when they see sales declining yet cut marketing? They don't see the need for marketing because "everyone already knows who our company is." Yep, that's actually happened. The cause is a lack of betterment in one or more processes of a product or service, and abolishing marketing so that products are more profitable is not going to fix it. A well-defined marketing strategy that is inclusive of all teams impacted will show you the gaps and more easily allow you to get at the root cause of declining sales.

For our next point we must assume that all other assumptions of the marketing manager and decision makers are accurate. Factoring this, something most managers don't understand is that marketing dollars have more criteria at play than the dollar value placed on them. Most marketing departments are told that their efforts need to generate more revenue than they put out via that expense line.

This notion only factors in the benefit of marketing that is bringing in interested parties to the sales and buying process. This isn't the only benefit marketing holds, however. Other benefits include building brand and reputation, embedding the idea of products and services into the fabric of communities, and increasing the perception of the company's culture and impact on the world.

All of these are intangibles that aren't easily trackable in terms of dollar amounts and it is important to note that the line between marketing and sales often becomes blurred. When marketing is asked to be a revenue source, as opposed or in addition to being strategic and supportive in nature, its actually not being acknowledged for what it brings to the sales team, who then get the revenue added to their statistics instead. Without risking confusion, it is possible to create revenue streams within marketing, but do so with caution and in tandem with sales. Not seeing them as two independent departments who have no overflow.

Clearly if a marketing department is far over budget and not in any reasonable range of breaking even from a revenue perspective something needs to change. However, if a company is putting out $50,000 in marketing, and they can directly measure $50,000 dollars of revenue coming back into the business from the marketing efforts, the betterment model would say that that marketing department has brought more than $50,000 worth of value to the business.

That isn't the view of many organizations that see $50,000, have a minimum needed return of 200% and don't see the value in the marketing team and the work they are doing.

Make sure you and your team are acknowledging and putting a value on intangibles that marketing is creating that impacts the sustainability and longevity of a business's perceived value in its locations of business.

Rule #5: Marketing Is Always Truthful And Transparent.

In life, lies eventually always come to truth. If they dont they can wear on a human's (and business') mental and emotional states. The bigger the lie, the more destruction it can create. While this seems like common sense and logical, we unfortunately ignore this basic ethical principle in reality too often.

In the marketing world this is no exception. Making claims and hiding truth about products or services to try to negate the negatives of a buyers decision making process will wear on a company's reputation.

It isn't only the customers who speak up and deteriorate a businesses good standing. When employees start to sense that something shady is happening within the company and their marketing tactics, their moral compass kicks in. This doesn't allow them to perform their jobs at an optimal level of commitment to the company's well being.

If important community members find out a product or service is being intentionally deceptive, it can spell huge trouble.

The best policy in marketing is ALWAYS truth and transparency, even at the expense of sales numbers. It will save you and make you money in the long run.

And, while the impact on larger companies is obviously at a different level, especially if products are national or even global, the smaller local businesses see micro impacts that add up over time and are felt closer to home.

There you have it. The 5 betterment rules for marketing. Easy, right? Follow these in your marketing efforts, planning and campaigning and your company will be a well running, profitable, bright light in the world.

12. BETTERMENT SALES

If you have a valid and high quality product that makes lives better and you have adopted the betterment mindset throughout your leadership and management, yet still are not seeing sales increase, it could be that sales is the single biggest component of business that is holding your company back from its fullest potential. So what happens when everyone in your company says, "I'm just not a sales guy." ?

Well, first, let's discuss the current perception of sales.

We all know a business or have seen one that portrays or has team members that portray the stereotypical slimy salesman. Those people holding sales positions often carry with them characteristics of only being about the sale, the quota and the commission. There seems to be a lack of compassion or understanding about the customers needs. Being driven only by numbers alone means a loss in the integrity of the customer relationship. How does this happen? Is it far from reality? No, it's not far from reality and it happens when the sales process and sales priorities are set up and executed within a company under the growth mindset.

The perception is that sales people are motivated by quotas with matching commissions. The higher volume they sell, meeting quotas, the higher their income. It becomes their driving factor and it becomes about the sale of the product. The customer and company values can get lost in the process under this model of business.

The resulting consequence is often at the expense of the customer. Because it becomes about the sale at all costs and not about the actual needs of the customer. The customer is often cajoled, convinced with perhaps not the best intentions, and pressured into buying whatever the product is that is being sold. And, trust us when we say, customers do figure this out and will ultimately leave.

We see salespeople resort to all kinds of tactics just to make that sale. Gone is the authenticity and even their own belief in the product and how it actually can make the lives of the right customers better in some way.

And, going even deeper, the sales person is at the mercy of the "sales plan." And, often this plan includes *only* performance evaluations based on the actual number of sales and not anything close to evaluations of the loyalty or satisfaction of the customer based on the salesperson. In fact, often times resulting repercussions come into play when a sales person doesn't meet a designated quota.

Now, understandably so, it's important for the growth

and stability of a company to ask for sales people to meet certain, attainable goals based on realistic projections and budgets. We do, of course, have overhead obligations that must be met.

And, in defense of the important salesperson and sales position, they are driven by the company plan, not by their own personality or authenticity. They are people walking into situations of rejection on literally a daily basis. And, sometimes, find themselves unable to communicate effectively with customers in a way that builds loyalty and integrity on behalf of the company.

However, wouldn't you agree that sustained growth, in the long run, is virtually unachievable with only this approach. It is vital to take the perspective of the customer into account and put it into play.

The business betterment movement means re-evaluating your sales process, your sales positions and the types of attributes you are looking for in your sales team.

Going back to the values of your business. What attributes and characteristics are important to you and a part of that overall culture? Integrity? Answering these questions again or simply going back to your previous answers will help you to gain perspective you need to define and build an effective and authentic sales process and team with the betterment mindset and your customers as a priority.

The key to solid sales that grows and betters your company, team, culture, and more is based on something you have read in previous chapters and will continue to see in upcoming chapters. Authenticity. There is really no other way to excel above the rest other than authenticity. Authenticity works so well because it is appealing to the right customer base. This doesn't just mean telling the truth about yourself, your company, and the products you're selling. It means delivering the message with transparency as we discussed in the marketing chapter. Most companies want to be authentic and think they are. Bust the truth is most companies just aren't. Again, not because they don't want to be, but because they haven't dove deep enough into their company values to really know what authenticity means for their business. On the other hand, if a company is too afraid or too nervous to be completely open about the product or service, it's time to re-evaluate. You and your sales staff should be proud to represent your company and its products and services openly and with transparency. If you aren't, or don't fully understand your company identity, then you aren't selling a product based on betterment or of being the ultimate service to your customer.

What is the purpose of sales? There's the obvious purpose of bringing in revenue, but that's really done through educating prospective customers. And that takes someone who is personable and very knowledgeable about your company and its products and services.

When did sales become so impersonal? Most sales teams and positions have one goal: meet a quota regardless of the outcome. Do you know where this model stems from? A fear of rejection: "If I don't care, it won't hurt" That isn't brave, that isn't authentic and it sure as heck isn't profitable in the long-term. This comes from a lack of education in conflict resolution and taking "no" personally. It also comes from a lack of passion for the product or service. Let's put an end to that.

Here are the five betterment rules for sales.

Rule #1: The Purpose Of Sales Is Never To Disorient, Distract Or Deceive To Make Money. Ever.

There is a common stereotype in sales of the "used car salesman." And while this stereotype seems most prevalent in auto sales, it is present in every industry to a degree. A company who is intentionally selling a product that they know isn't best for the prospective customers simply to fill a sales quota is not putting the customer above all else or even being true to their defined values. That is the very definition of a company centered on growth and not betterment. Now this can be a product that we refer to as complete "snake oil" or it can be a product that is right for some people but not for others. If there are not enough people that truly want or need a product that are willing to buy it, where the company feels they have to trick those who don't need or want the product into buying it to reach a sustainable level of revenue, then the product and business model *need* to be reassessed for betterment. Sadly, the action taken is usually to push more sales, ignoring ethical boundaries rather than bettering their business model.

The most important aspect of sales is honesty. This also applies to what we talked about earlier which is not being upfront and honest about what your product truly does. Exaggerating the capabilities and the benefits of your product or service in order to gain customers is the same disconnect with betterment by pushing your product on to customers who really don't need it and just aren't the right customers.

This is not only a stereotype, but it is something those of us who are ethical and conscious-minded companies have to battle because there are many companies that caused distrust among their customer based which has indirectly impacted all of us. When this happens we all work harder to gain that loyalty and trust. Like the saying goes, "one bad apple can spoil the whole bunch."

The only way to repair the world-wide perception of business sales is one lead at a time. By making processes and sales systems that are authentic, based on empathy and curiosity of a potential customers' needs we can change the perception of business (and increase our conversion rates). It takes thoughtfulness, integrity and honest communication and it can be done.

In our model, the only way to build trust authentically is through honesty. There is no other way. This doesn't just mean telling the truth, it also means you shouldn't conceal any relevant facts about your products or services from your customer base and even your team. If there is something you are fearful of them knowing or finding out about your product, then you aren't selling a product based on betterment or being of ultimate service to your customers and, in our belief, your company should not be selling that particular product or service.

The main purpose of sales *is* to always bring in more revenue by educating potential customers and current customers on the benefits of your product that resonate with their needs and wants, resulting in the purchase of a product or service. Sales is an educational tool that builds relationships by explaining who the product or service is for, but also who it isn't for. Ultimately if your sales team and trainings aren't focused on betterment, your business will suffer the consequences and lack sustainable growth.

If this is not the main objective of sales in your company, no matter how high your sales numbers, you are not doing sales for betterment.

It is that simple.

If the benefits of your product or service do not appeal to someone, it's because:

> *It isn't a good fit for them right now.*
> *or,*

> *They can't afford it.*
> *or,*

> *It wasn't explained or sold in a way that they understood how it benefits them.*

The only one of these that you can have a direct and immediate impact on is how you explain and sell your product. You cannot force a product or service to be right for someone. You cannot magically make consumers have more money in the moment. So focus on the third and don't take a "no" personally. Speaking of which, keep reading and take note of Rule #2.

Rule #2: "No" Is Not A Reflection Of Your Company.

But constructive criticism from getting those "no" answers is incredibly valuable and an opportunity to gain insight about your products. It can give you insight on how they can be better, how you can expand your market, what other products and services you can provide, or be an acknowledgement of your current products and services and how they are working for customers.

That being said, sales isn't about collecting "no's" until you get a "yes". It's always about being of service and the best customer service you are capable of providing.

That doesn't mean you won't collect "no's," but it is a reframe. "No's" are simply people or companies who either didn't understand the value or didn't understand your product or service. Or, potentially, they did understand fully, assessed, and decided it wasn't for them. That means one opportunity is that you can learn how to better communicate the value, but understand that beyond that a "no" means "the product is not for me," not, "I don't like you or your product." This is important because, if you adopt this mindset, you fully understand that a "no" is not a reflection of anything wrong or a negative rejection of your business. As long as you, your products and your services are there to truly make life or business better, you are simply showing what you have to offer and finding who is a good fit by sifting through the majority of the population.

Rule #3: Sales Should Always Be Personal.

Don't think this rule means you can throw #2 out the window. While sales is personal, that doesn't mean it needs to be *taken* personally. There is a difference that we will explain further

Sales is a chance for someone to get to know and understand your business and your company. Even if they are not your customer, they leave feeling connected and good about your business being in the world.

Marketing can be generalized, but once someone is aware of your product or service, it becomes sales. And it becomes personal. This awareness comes with a curiosity of wondering if your product or service works for them and if they can incorporate it into their life or business to make it even better. This is always done through personal relationships. Even if the sale is happening digitally and without human contact, you are still making a personal connection through emails, phone calls, your website and your online social media presence.

Think about this as you consider airlines and the travel industry in general and how their sales process works. Many airlines and other travel businesses such as cruise lines, work hard to create a connection with their customers during the sales process. More often than not, the most interaction a customer will have within this industry while purchasing or looking to purchase is on the phone with a representative. The familiarity generally comes through online research and social presence in creating those connections.

This is one of the reasons videos have become so huge in sales. This is why Amazon.com, even though the site isn't the most stunning we have seen, has such high continual and return sales volumes. Going to Amazon.com has an emotional and exciting, personal experience for many individuals.

Creating this type of feeling in your sales efforts can pay off in dividends whether it is through in-person contact or otherwise. It's all still personal.

Rule #4: Sales Requires Bravery, But Can Easily Turn Into Cunningness For Those Who Aren't Strong Enough To Accept Failure Or Rejection.

The solution is not complex. Learn to gracefully accept rejection. Know that it isn't about you or your company. Learn to not take it personally. But as we just said in Rule #3, sales *is* personal.

This takes bravery. Standing in front of one person or one thousand and getting laughed at, ridiculed or rejected can feel like a degrading experience. Our feelings and perceptions about these circumstances defines us and is what makes it a degrading experience. If we truly understand that positive criticism and critique is one of our single biggest allies, and negative or unhelpful criticism and critique is not a reflection of us but the attitude and perception of someone else experiencing pain or fear, we can let go of the hold it has on us.

This transformative process is one of the most freeing and impactful personal growth opportunities that sales has to offer us. It is such a fulfilling part of sales from a personal growth perspective. Here is a statement that has helped us remember this numerous times in our multiple businesses:

> *What you think, feel, and say defines you 100%, how someone reacts or responds to that defines them 100%. Reversely, what someone thinks, feels and says defines them 100%. How you react and respond to that defines you 100%.*

Read this over a few times and really think about its meaning. Live this and become a master of sales.

Rule #5: Nothing In Business Will Have A Chance To Become Better Without Sales.

No matter how much interest you build or awareness you build about your products and services, if you are not directly offering it to people on a macro and micro level, digitally or physically, then your company cannot and will not grow. It is the single biggest leaky hole a company can have.

Some products and services go viral or get endorsed by important people or companies. This referral network can help. However, if people cannot easily interact to buy or inquire about what you have to offer, it won't make a long-term difference.

There is no other department whose energy and time output have the capabilities to make a bigger impact on revenue than sales. Understanding this can help you or your company take the leap to reaching out more and more to potential clients, even long-shots.

Your sales process needs to reflect the above betterment rules. Build them into your sales process and trainings and see the difference for yourself.

In the next chapter we will discuss the Customer Experience, bringing together the importance of connecting the customer to your product, your business and all of your sales and marketing activities.

13. BETTERMENT CUSTOMER EXPERIENCE

C ustomer experience is the crux that can lift your products and services to greatness or make the highest quality companies crumble under the weight of customer outrage at underperforming customer care.

Your customer experience includes every step in the process that a prospective customer interacts with in your business. That includes but is not limited to (takes deep breath) your online processes that customers interact with, your storefront, your store layout, your customer wait times, your call service or centers, scheduling, record keeping, and your data management.

Anything that a customer has an opportunity to have an opinion or interaction with is involved in their overall experience, and coincidently your overall brand.

I know it seems big and all-encompassing, but you really

only have to remember one thing when it comes to customer experience; above and beyond.

We would like to use the Ritz-Carlton as an example of "above and beyond". Did you know that they instituted a policy that staff could spend up to $2000 to make guests happy? This was implemented alongside the policy of taking 10-minute meetings where staff shares "wow" stories from each other of how they helped customers. As you could imagine, with that level of empowerment, there could be a lot of pretty phenomenal examples of customer care. Those stories include such examples as having an employee fly internationally to personally deliver a lost laptop to a customer.

Now, most businesses don't have this level of resources. However, the point of this story isn't the level of expense the company spent to make guests have an above and beyond experience. The point of the example as a whole is the level of importance and priority the Ritz-Carlton places on that experience. Over a year, they are spending quite a pretty penny making customers happy. That is money that could be going to executive bonuses, expansion and much more. But instead, they *choose* to spend it on customer experience.

You only need one of two things to increase customer experience in your business; time or money. If you and your team contribute both, even better. Regardless of how much you have of each, the five rules below will help you use the time and money your business does have on customer experience to the fullest.

Rule #1: Curiosity Eclipses Judgement.

Judgment is what happens when a customer is complaining about a particular product, service, or representative and they get met with skepticism or indifference.

We understand that a team member may be having a bad day and that particular customer was just one too many, but on average, everyone and everything in your organization should be interacting with customers in the spirit of curiosity and helpfulness. At every level of the organization, and in every process (automated help, logins, online systems, kiosks...) this should be true.

Curiosity is essentially an empathy for another individual, in this case a customer, that allows you to use emotional intelligence to understand their situation and how they came to be in their emotional state, or their conclusions (no matter how "wrong" they are.)

If every customer at every stage of their customer lifecycle was treated with pure curiosity and empathy, what would be different about your company's customer satisfaction?

Rule #2: Build A Tribe.

If you think about your own life, it's possible to think about the people in your inner circle as your "tribe" right? Your tribe of good friends, family, and supporters. Those are the people you most rely on. It's absolutely necessary that we have those people in our lives. And it's absolutely necessary that we have those people in our business environment as well.

Don't fall in the pit that can occur using the growth mindset. From this mindset, "tribalism" can be used as a phrase in today's media to describe the mentality of groups of people doing their own thing and isolating others. When an isolation attitude or an "us versus them" mentality takes over, it negates that whole idea of a support system. When this happens, it can literally erode morale which then impacts your entire organization.

It's important to keep a very inclusionary thought and environment when building a tribe and not succumbing to alienating groups of your core support network.

Rule #3: Know What Your Customers Want Next (Before They Do).

Many products that we consume or purchase in life we don't actually need. We actually have very few basic needs. Everything else is a want. Most of the time, we don't know we want something until we see it, hear about it or feel it. This could be a movie preview, a product that fulfills a want that we didn't know was possible, or learning about a way to feed our inner nerd with a new widget or technology.

There are people and companies out there whose primary competitive advantage is their ability to track trends and wants before they happen. Or at the very least, adapt to wants and trends as they are happening quicker than other companies.

That isn't to say these companies are batting a 100% average. They are comfortable with trying and failing if a trend or want doesn't go a certain way. Just keep that in mind as you try to shine your crystal ball.

Do your customers want more digital offerings? Are they reclusing from the digital era and craving more physical and brick and mortar options? You need to know the right questions to ask for your market and industry. With the right questions, you can find the right answers. With the right answers, you can know what your customers want next before they do.

Rule #4: Loyal Customers Always Become Team Members.

Customers have the potential to expand your marketing reach without any extra effort on the company's end. They tell friends, family, acquaintances at the store, people they meet on the plane, their social media followings, and sometimes anyone they can, about your products and services. The better the experience, the better the product, the more positive the conversation.

These loyal customers are generated naturally by your customer experience efforts. It is near impossible to *try* to create loyal customers. But knowing they exist based on your efforts, and why their existence is important, can be the motivation a team member needs to go that extra mile for a difficult customer.

Speaking of difficult customers, it has been our experience that, somehow by the laws of the universe, when you finally do make them satisfied, they are more loyal than any other customer you could imagine. They typically become a doorway to their entire social circle. Sorry that they can't just be nice or go away. But in the end, your company's bank account will be glad they didn't. Just some more food for thought!

Rule #5: There Is No Neutral Customer.

Every customer is on a scale of positive or negative experience. There is no neutral experience, there is no neutral customer.

If people have an "okay" experience, it means that they experienced something of benefit but there was still something that made the experience less than enjoyable. They may return once or twice, but ultimately the negatives will weigh on them and make the experience not worth returning to. Just like in a personal relationship, the longer you are with someone the more their "faults," or in other words, the things that irritate you about them, no matter how small, have more of an emotional impact.

The best remedy for neutral customers is communication and, again, going above and beyond. Send them a gift basket. Express appreciation. Ask them for their opinion. What do these actions have in common? They all show curiosity or empathy for who they are as a person and customer. This will always pay off; either by saving you a negative review, extending that customer's sales cycle in your business, or creating a loyal customer. No matter what the outcome, it is worth the effort.

With these five rules ingrained in your company's team, you will be able to build an above and beyond customer experience. Be curious. Be helpful. Rinse. Repeat. These rules will become second nature in the back of everyone's mind. Once they are, responses and interactions will automatically add value to the brand and services that you offer. Now go build a tribe!

14. ONE'S OWN

While this is a business book, the betterment business movement is also about you! Authenticity, doing the right thing, focusing on the needs of others and creating a contribution are not only about business but are also not entirely possible to achieve without focusing on your energy sustainability and output.

Self-care and life-balance are terms that we are all very familiar with in this day and age. There are a lot of definitions and thoughts of practice when it comes to these terms. And, really, when it comes to your own life and business, it becomes more about what works for you regardless of what the general biological science says.

Have you ever noticed a co-worker or colleague that is obviously unhappy? Most people have, if not for noticing it in ourselves at some point in time. When someone is chronically unhappy, whether it be in their personal lives or in their professional lives, it impacts virtually everything around them. You've recognized these people as the ones with lacking contribution and focus, lack of compassion, and even a persistent pessimism.

When there is a disconnect with who we are as people, it can create a disconnect with many of the aspects of business. If we find ourselves unsure or unclear about direction or purpose, it can leave us with that feeling of floundering and not being able to engage in our work the way we truly want to.

Every member of your company matters in that they are there to serve a function. That function is performed based on their performance. Their performance directly relates to their physical appearance, mental, and emotional health. These things *should* matter to the business because they *directly affect it*. Every company should find a balance by actively supporting their team members to keep a balanced life without breaking the company bank.

Have you ever heard of the concept of a wounded healer? It's when humans focus on giving more to others than they physically have the capacity for or overwork themselves in order to avoid their own personal care. They give so much that they literally have nothing left in their energy reserves, eventually burn out, feel resentful for those they care for or are giving to, and in the end have nothing to give in the long term. As a leader it is not sustainable to give everything you have and not give to yourself. By incorporating self care and encouraging others in your organization to do the same, you will have more to give to your company for a longer period of time. It's that simple.

While most of us inherently know what it is that we want and need to do to be healthy, we still don't do it.

Jesse, through one of his other businesses, has created a system for those who fit in this category. It also works for those who don't have a clue where to start and need some prompting to see how to move forward. The system is called the Holistic Health Canvas.

If you have studied business in recent times, you are probably aware of the Business Model Canvas that conveys the flow, operations and organization of a business and allows you and your team to communicate all components effectively. The Holistic Health Canvas is similar.

By organizing your thoughts about your health and life in a one-page format that you can refer to often, you will be able to more easily connect with the WHY of your self care and remember how your efforts affect your personal and professional career.

Here is what the canvas looks like:

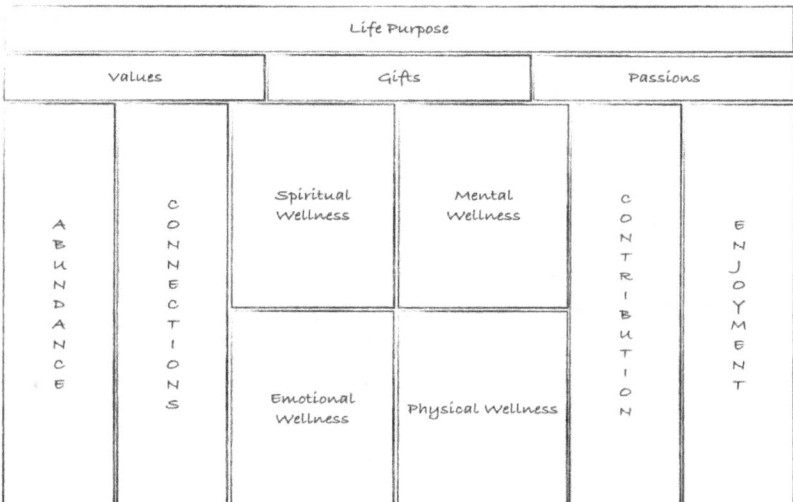

Throughout the rest of the chapter, we will be going through this Holistic Health Model section-by-section to give you an idea of what is involved in each section.

The first four components are usually on a subconscious level and on auto pilot for most people. These factors determine whether you are experiencing primarily joy, or primarily internal pain, stress or anxiety.

Purpose

Your purpose refers to WHY you are here in this world, what you *believe* you are here to do or experience, and how you are meant to show up to those experiences. It's not *what* you want to do, but it's *how* you want to show up in any given situation of your life. The question is, "Who do I feel I am meant to be in this moment?" and clarifying that as often as possible. Let's be clear, as a conscious process this can be exhausting at first. But you are literally already doing this on a subconscious level and simply not giving yourself a concious choice about it. It's happening wether you want it to or not.

Every time that you act, respond or react to a situation you are doing so through how you believe you are supposed to react based on what you believe about yourself and your purpose in the situation.

This is important in business and in life because if you change what you believe about your purpose, you can change your interactions with people. And people, in general, are the main way we feel supported when we are at a low and they contribute to our successes when we are at our best. The reason this is true is because almost everything we do in life and every major challenge we need to overcome requires other people. Have you ever needed help with a business license error? Or a shipment went rouge and you needed to track it down? Have you ever thought about how many people were involved in making the book, tablet or speakers with which you are consuming this content?

Everything in our urban and suburban life requires human contact. Simply by shifting your focus onto changing your interactions based on your purpose, you will find interactions with others to be more rewarding in business and easier to navigate, and as a leader potentially create more internal ownership for employees to your business.

If you want to approach your team members to engage in these question for themselves, ask them how they would like to show up in their job and life if they were being their ideal self. You may have to massage the conversation a bit, but once answered, it will allow you to hold them accountable for that and leverage their ideal to create a more productive, thoughtful employee. This helps you and them in the process.

Values

There are really two sets of values that are important, and have slightly different definitions.

The first is what most of us would think of when we

hear the word values. A handful of words and their definitions that we individually believe are the most important characteristics to uphold. These are called our **conscious values**.

These conscious values allow you to give yourself a direction for your purpose. If you define *how* you want to show up in any given situation, these handful of conscious values and their definitions give you a tangible roadmap to experiencing your purpose.

The second definition is essentially the way we inherently act and perceive the world when we wake up in the morning or are on "auto-pilot". These are called our **core values**.

There are four core values that then have different characteristics in terms of conflict strategy, learning style, ways of approaching tasks and tasks that each core value finds the most energizing.

What this has allowed our clients to do is better understand how to communicate and give motivating incentives to those around them, as well as understand their conflict strategies and be able to adapt them for better leadership and management results.

We have a link on our website, www.thenticate.biz, to a free core values-based assessment that can give you all of the information you need about your core values and how they affect your life. This may help offer some insight into this area of your life if it isn't entirely clear to you already.

Gifts

Your gifts are the things that you are naturally good at. It's not necessarily what you like, but it's the qualities and tasks and information that you have natural inclinations for that make you unique as an individual.

The more we use these gifts in our life and business, the easier and more efficient it becomes. We can gain more clarity for identifying these gifts easily through the core value assessment process.

Now, life isn't always about efficiency and some of your gifts may not be things you enjoy doing all the time even though you are naturally good at them, but even so it is nice to know and acknowledge the things that are gifts so that we can leverage them when we want to or need to.

It is also nice to know the gifts of those in our organization that we work closely with, and help them identify their gifts so that you can utilize them to their highest potential where it aligns with their role.

Passions

Your passions are the things that you love to do EVEN if you are not good at them. Here, we aren't focused on success and betterment but simple, pure enjoyment.

But, how is this important to business? Because balance is important to business; in employee retention, in employee burnout, and in us as managers and leaders to maintain our energy level and clarity on important decisions. We need things outside of work that we are passionate about at times when we just aren't feeling that passion in our business.

Also, knowing the passions of your team members allows you to reward and incentivize them in unique ways, which then allows for a deeper connection and commitment to you as a leader and to the business.

When you put together your purpose, passions, gifts and values on a regular basis, as well as understand those of your team members, it is impossible not to feel a higher level of fulfillment and it is completely possible to increase the success of your business through stronger relationships and understanding of them.

The next two One's Own factors are called **indicators**. They allow you to indicate how fulfilled you are at any given moment in time.

Abundance Indicator

The first indicator is about abundance. The question here is, "How abundant am I feeling right now?" Assuming that abundance in this world can be our natural state of being, when we aren't feeling abundant, we are closed off from something. This indicates that there needs to be a shift, probably in one of the areas below, assuming that we are clear about our values, passions, gift and purpose.

Enjoyment Indicator

The second indicator is enjoyment. Enjoyment is, well, enjoyment. Your level of enjoyment indicates how connected you are with the flow and natural state of life. Our natural state is one of joy and enjoyment in life. Stress, anxiety, scarcity, sadness and the like are all learned conditions based on our experience. Coincidently, they can be habits and patterns we develop and not actually indicative of our current reality. These learned conditions can be more so an automated response to familiar situations. As we work through the following areas of One's Own, we will be able to increase our level of enjoyment consistently as we increase our satisfaction in each one of these areas; contribution, connection with others, physical wellness, emotional wellness, mental wellness and spiritual wellness.

You can also use this area to jot down the things in life you do for pure enjoyment, if those things weren't already listed in your passions.

Contribution

Your contribution is your career or mission in life. It also pertains to any volunteer work that you feel adds to that mission or your overall purpose. So what you would do here is make a list of all of the things you *do* (or want to do) that make a contribution to making this world a better place than you found it both for supporting yourself financially and that you do for others without return. Then, you would describe how those activities make you feel and if there is anything you wish could be different about your primary contributions.

Decide how satisfied you feel with these, and if there are any simple actions that can be made to increase satisfaction for your current contribution in life.

Connections

We connect in life with all of the people around us. We do this in different ways depending on our role and the relationship of the individual or group. There are six major categories we distinguish in terms of connections; family, friendships, intimate relationships, parenting, working relationships and acquaintances.

It isn't necessarily about the quantity, or even the quality of these relationships in your life. It is more about how you feel about these relationships and what you want in relation to what you feel you have. If you feel you are lacking in any of these human categories of connection, those are categories where your perception or feeling is taking energy away from your present enjoyment.

Next, we look at the four different types of internal wellness, starting with physical wellness.

Physical Wellness

This is probably the most widely understood, and over-focused area of health there is. It is also the most acted on. The five categories we would put under physical wellness are...

1. Rest and relaxation
2. Movement and activity
3. Nutrition
4. Pain management
5. Hygiene

All of these are important and contribute to the overall physical health of us as individuals.

If we are lacking in commitment or execution to one or more of these, we can start to see the effects in every other aspect of our life. This is actually true about every area we discuss here in one's own chapter, so keep that in mind as we continue to move through.

Mental (Brain) Wellness

This isn't about psychology, but more about how optimized and healthy your brain is to perform the way you need it to perform, process and communicate throughout the day. There are seven areas for you to test and rate to determine how well your brain is performing in comparison to who you want it to:

1. Memory
2. Focus
3. Clarity
4. Problem solving
5. Decision making
6. Communication
7. Flexibility

How well you feel your brain performs in these functions is your mental wellness health assessment. There are sites you can go to, such as luminosity.com, for a "mental wellness" or "brain age" assessment. To help you be a bit more accurate and statistical with this information. The brain operates as a muscle, so the good news is you can get better at any of these areas over time if you practice and challenge them. A lot of times in our work we use a few of them consistently to perform, but do not challenge some others. Brain wellness can also be affected heavily by emotional and physical wellness which release certain hormones and chemicals that can either positively or negatively change how well we perform in the seven areas of brain wellness.

Emotional Wellness

Emotional wellness determines how well we interact with others through the management and use of emotional stability. We do this through five areas:

1. Emotional intelligence
2. Emotional awareness
3. Emotional expression
4. Emotion connection
5. Stress management

Because stress is an epidemic in our culture and a leading contributor to disease and death around the world, we specifically want to talk about the fact that there are two types of stress that need to be managed. We denote these as **anabolic stress** and **catabolic stress**.

Anabolic stress is stress that is used to build yourself up. So when we are learning something new, using a part of our brain we don't often use, or when we are moving and working out brain muscles more than usual we are stretching those parts of ourselves in the process to build them back up stronger than before. What we are doing is challenging ourselves to become better. The challenge is the stress, but the outcome is the betterment. In a balanced manner, anabolic stress can be beneficial, even on a daily basis. However, overstress or over-stimulation can and will lead to burnout, even if it is anabolic. We cannot be challenging our minds and our bodies every second of every day and expect them not to deteriorate faster from a lack of rest and relaxation.

Catabolic stress breaks us down and, in the long term, can be very harmful. In the short term what it does is break down components of your body to be used immediately. It is not the healthiest way, but is most certainly the most efficient way in a stressful or intense moment that *needs* to be handled with the utmost focus and physical power. This could mean helping others out of a burning building, a bomb squad team using catabolic stress to figure out how to disarm a live bomb, avoiding an oncoming accident, etc. In these circumstances, catabolic stress is a perfectly normal response. What it allows your body to do is pump more blood and oxygen to your muscles and brain to perform at a higher level, at the expense of flooding our bodies with adrenaline and other hormones. This, in your everyday setting, is not an appropriate response to stressful situations that are not life or death. It is, unfortunately, the most common response to stress because it is the easiest and most addictive way to access motivation and energy.

If we can begin to frame more situations in our life in the anabolic form of stress for betterment we can, overtime with the goal of sustainably, build our body and mind up ina powerful way. We can then also decrease the amount of negative symptoms we experience from *far* too much catabolic stress; adrenal fatigue, weight gain, hormonal imbalances, and much worse.

Spiritual Wellness

Spiritual wellness refers to how you connect with whatever it is that you believe in. Regardless of your personal beliefs, there are three ways that anyone in any belief can connect with that part of themselves more effectively in whatever one might believe in;

1. Devotion
2. Inspiration
3. Action.

Devotion

Devotion is whatever you use in life to connect with and express gratitude for what you believe in. For an atheist this may be connecting with nature or scientific principles and expressing gratitude for the one experience they are having in the universe. For a christian this could look like a quick gratitude before meals, and allowing the Holy Spirit to "take the wheel" in certain situations of their life. In any case, it is how you devote yourself to connecting with the source of your choice; the universe, God(s), or whatever else you may believe in. How do you connect internally with what you believe in in an active way?

Contemplation

Contemplation is the meditation, visualization and study of what you believe in or are exploring to potential belief in. Here, we reflect on what we learn and intuitively feel about existence and we expand our knowledge on that *through* deepening our understanding.

Devotion is about *connecting* with or *experiencing* your spiritual belief. Contemplation is about deepening your *understanding* and *learning* about your spiritual belief.

Action

Action is the dedication to creating and maintaining space in your life, either through a space in your home, nature or somewhere else where you connect with the world in a spiritual way. Some people do this through hiking, having a meditation room, going to spiritual groups on a periodic basis of their comfort level, and connecting with others one-on-one or in groups. Spiritual **action** is the steps one takes in their life to commit to making the time and space for **contemplation** and **devotion**.

Spiritual wellness is important for many reasons. We are not preaching any one form of religion or spiritual belief. And like we have already expressed, we are not saying anyone has to believe in a higher power to find spiritual wellness important. But we believe that spiritual wellness applies even to those who have a belief in nothing, or a belief that we can never truly know *why* we are here, and so do not form spiritual or religious beliefs. This is because in order to truly know and commit to a belief or non-belief, one must have taken the time to form these beliefs and learn about other beliefs to understand that those beliefs are not for them. The more time that is taken in these efforts, the more certain we feel about our own reality and understanding of why we are here. Whether this time makes us feel that we know more about the universe or less about it, it is still time taken that feeds our inner need for understanding and exploration. That is the heart of what we mean and why we feel spiritual wellness is an important factor in how abundant we feel, how fulfilled we feel and how much enjoyment we feel in life. It is equally important to mental, physical and emotional wellness and our business betterment.

◆ ◆ ◆

Influencers

Now that you have a personal view of the aspects of life that affect our overall success and satisfaction that are completely within our control to shift, we aren't quite finished. There are three influential factors that can affect, positively or negatively, our overall wellness that aren't exactly a part of our Holistic Health Canvas. The reason they aren't technically a part of the main canvas of your health is that they aren't as easily changed or shifted in life. That is, they are more concrete and sometimes a completely fixed point. They are things that influence our health, hence the name **influencers**. These are the three areas of influence;

1. Inspiration

This is essentially how often we are "given" solutions to creatively solve health, business or other challenges. Sometimes we want to get healthy, for example in physical wellness, and even with all the tools and knowledge we can't think of any way we feel inspired to actually improve our health in a sustainable or exciting way. We cannot force these intuitive hits. No one can. We can find ways to access them more, like some of the great minds of our time have, but it is still not something we can often access or control by the snap of a finger.

The only ways we have found to consistently access inspiration more often is by increasing our true feeling of abundance and enjoyment in life. This is done by better understanding our purpose, values, gifts and passions. Also by taking action towards the things that will make us feel more physically, mentally, emotionally and spiritually satisfied. Also by connecting more with the type of people we want, less with the people we don't and contributing to the world in more ways that we wish to. Alas, this is one of the major benefits to understanding and utilizing the Holistic Health Canvas. The more you use it, the more inspired you feel in general, the more you can move forward creatively and with ease, and therefore the more it becomes an upward spiral of abundance and enjoyment in life.

168 | F*CK GROWTH

For example, let's say that we decide we want to focus on our mental wellness. We know that our mind isn't as healthy as we want it to be. However, when we look at the prompts and research and information for how to help our brain be more healthy, nothing really resonates or strikes a chord. We then try to sit down and write out some ways to build our brain muscle and we draw a blank. Yet, someone else could immediately find an exercise or plan for strengthening their brain that resonates with them and that allows them to move forward and create an action plan in moments.

The more confident we are in our ability to connect with inspiration, the easier we can access it, but don't feel bad or down if you struggle at points to draw inspiration in your life or business. Inspiration will still always be a fickle friend.

2. Environment

Environment includes economic, home, seasonal and relationship environments. Some of these we can change by moving, but uprooting our lives takes a significant amount of effort and that isn't always reasonable. For example, your body may not love humid weather, and it actually decreases your physical wellness at times but that one factor isn't enough for you to move away from the family, friends and a job that you love.

On the other hand, if you find out your current residence has a major black mold issue, you are more than likely going to move right away. So in some ways these areas are controllable, but because of other factors you may be more likely just to live with them than to go through the discomfort of changing them.

For those reasons, environment has an influence on your overall wellness but often it takes more energy, time and resources than simply deciding to do something different in your environment to change it quickly.

3. External Blocks

External blocks are the parts of your life that affect your ability to reach your goals that you may have little control over. The first external block is **time**. We all have the same amount of time in a day. We cannot change that. We also have no idea when our time on this earth is going to come to an end, but we do know that our time in this body is limited. We can, however, effect how we *use* time. That is the only way we can manipulate this influencer for our betterment.

The second area of external block is **resources**. All resources on the earth are finite. We can gain more or less but not all of them. These include space, money and assets. What you currently have in these areas affects your ability to do what you want to do or change what you want to change. If you want to buy a private jet, but have $10 in your bank account, that is a resource problem. That is an external block.

The third area of external block is our personal **constitution**. We are born into the body we have, and there is not much we can do to change the overall structure of it. If we are born without an arm, we can get a prosthetic one for the right amount of resources, but we can never wish ourselves to have a "normal" arm and be able to make it happen. At least not in our current level of scientific understanding. If someone wants to be the fastest running human alive, but has one lung and just had a knee replacement, that desire is being hindered by the external block of constitution.

We can reframe our desires, our thoughts and beliefs around external blocks, but we often cannot directly change them.

This, in summation, is everything you need to know to create a more comprehensive, holistic approach to wellness in terms of your work and life balance. By looking at each of these areas, constructing the micro details of each section and then stepping back to take a macro view of everything, you can see where and how you can make the biggest impacts in your life to experience more balance, abundance and enjoyment.

To start this process with each area of wellness, simply ask yourself these questions:

1. What is my current life like in regards to _____. (i.e. What is my current life like in regard to my connection to others?)

2. How satisfied am I with my current life in regards to _____?

3. What would make me feel 10% more satisfied? 30%? 50%?

If inspiration or motivation strikes you, you can create an action plan for moving forward. Of course, life is complicated and going at this alone can be complex, even if laid out simply. We tend to be our own worst enemies in that our mind can steer us away from what we want or need based on our own personal anxieties, fears, and trauma. If you are struggling, reach out to a friend, family member, coach or other professional to help you commit to and overcome anything holding you back from where you want to be in any of these areas of wellness.

You can download a full version of our Holistic Health Canvas at www.Thenticate.biz/resources to download for personal use.

Now that you have a tool for organizing your current health and personal goals, you can incorporate self-care into your business betterment strategy. Good luck and have fun!

PART 3

Betterment in Action

15. THE BETTERMENT MODEL

Business can be complex, and between all the areas of business you have learned 40 business betterment rules plus a holistic health model and then some.

In this chapter we have put all of the betterment rules in one place with brief summaries for your convenience or review. You can come back to this place in this book, find a specific betterment rule you resonate with easily, or to scan/copy it to put it in view for you to remember throughout your business day and for planning meetings.

You can also visit our website to download a graphically formatted versions of each set of betterment rules at www.thenticate.biz

Betterment Business Mindset

A efficient, effective and exceptional method of planning, growth and action in business that focuses on holistic and sustainable practices.

Operations

Key logistics, activities and administrative functions that internally produce products and services that best serve a team, customer and their community.

Rule #1: Slow, continuous improvement over a long period of time is the best approach to operations.

This is the definition of Kaizen. Growth in the extreme without the foundation necessary to do so is a business killer. It can also lead to crippling growing pains that produce "scars" that may be irreversible. Focus instead on incremental action that leads to the ultimate objective.

Rule #2: If you are focused on betterment, you must plan for growth.

This will limit the growing pains that can happen with growth. Growth which will happen if your business is focused on betterment.

Rule #3: Operations main focus is the quality and perfected execution for products and services with as little negative environmental and community impact as possible.

Think of this as the hippocratic oath that doctoral physicians take, but for all businesses.

Rule #4: Operations secondary focus is always customer and employee experience.

These are the main reasons and purpose that your product exists so beyond perfect execution, all planning and decisions should be done with these groups in mind.

Rule #5: Operations final focus is cost, compliance and communication.

Communication between departments, compliance with necessary (and beyond necessary) entities and how products and services affect the bottom-line of your company.

Products/Services

The key value created, packaged, and sold that solves, with passion, a need or want in the world.

Rule #1: Compete on quality and service, not cost.

Unless you are one of the biggest companies in the world who creates the cheapest, least expensive products and services, your customers factor quality and service more than cost in their decision making process, do focus on differentiating these.

Rule #2: Become a part of the solution.

The best and most sustainable products and services focus on passionately fulfilling deep needs and wants.

Rule #3: Realistically promise, over deliver.

Your product and service should realistically state its specific intent and value for the sake of customer research and knowledge, without over complication. However, every product and service has other benefits that are tangible and intangible that will add to the customers perceived value can over-deliver.

Rule #4: The best products and services start with a smart product and service development process.

Just like in painting, the majority of the work is in the prep. The more detailed and deep your development process, the better the product or service.

Rule #5: Always ask for and use customer feedback.

Don't just ask for it to check a box in the company systems. Use the customer feedback for real change and staying relevant.

Leadership

Strategic activities that navigate and direct the company at every level.

<u>Rule #1</u>: Every team member is a leader.

Leadership is a mindset that every team member can embody to reach the highest possible function of their particular role.

<u>Rule #2</u>: Leadership sets the tone for culture.

Culture is based on perception. Perception is based on actions observed. Actions are based on leadership decisions.

<u>Rule #3</u>: Leadership is flexible and factors holistically.

Leadership adapts to the situation and plans accordingly based on as many factors as possible.

<u>Rule #4</u>: Strategy is collaborative at its finest.

The more leaders and team member perceptions that can be collaborated with in decision making, the more holistic and solid the final decision will be.

<u>Rule #5</u>: Leadership is transparent.

Betterment leadership leaves everything out on the table and can easily show its process getting from "a" to "b" in crucial decisions made about the company.

Management

The inclusive oversight of resources and activity execution for furthering company objectives.

<u>Rule #1</u>: People are more important than objectives.

A Managers focus is on their team welfare first and *then* the objectives.

<u>Rule #2</u>: Dictatorship doesn't work.

Ruling with the "because I said so" mentality and asserting authority for the purpose of manipulation is a recipe for departmental disaster.

<u>Rule #3</u>: Management holds answers to operative betterment.

The more management observations that can be factored into operational decisions the better.

<u>Rule #4</u>: Objectives are expectations, not reality.

Objectives are made up numbers based on the best possible assumptions, but they are still assumptions that need to be handled with flexibility.

<u>Rule #5</u>: Managers are conduits.

They bridge together the officers and stakeholders with the people actually creating the value of the company. They are what allows the company to gain and use vital information for communication both ways.

Team

All of the people who support the fulfillment of company products and services.

<u>Rule #1</u>: Companies growing individuals grow individuals who grow companies.

The more a company invests in its people, the more benefit and value those people can bring to the company.

<u>Rule #2</u>: Your methods of finding and hiring the right people is an important intellectual property.

Invest in doing it right. The first time. One of the least efficient and most costly aspects of business is the investment in finding and training new talent.

<u>Rule #3</u>: Independent contractors, joint venture relationships and vendors are team members.

Anyone who supports the fulfillment of a product or service is a part of that business team.

<u>Rule #4</u>: "Team" includes personal and non-operative support networks.

For each individual, the support they receive is a business asset and a part of the business team. Just think, whether you know it or not, some of your employee's best ideas come from conversations with their significant others and family.

<u>Rule #5</u>: Effective team resource usage = efficient spending.

The more effectively you train and utilize your human resources, without burnout or dissatisfaction, the more efficiently you are spending your money on human resources which increases profitability.

Culture

The feeling and perception people get when thinking about the experiences they have with your company.

<u>Rule #1</u>: Culture must be based on the betterment of business and the individuals within.

When this is taken in action form, people will notice and their perception will change for the better. This changes the culture.

<u>Rule #2</u>: Culture is the spreading of ideas.

Ideas get spread through conversation and action. Actions create observations which form more ideas and opinions. These spread and continue the cycle.

<u>Rule #3</u>: Culture is not a tool to control subordinates.

It just isn't.

<u>Rule #4</u>: Culture is the single biggest factor in retention, loyalty and happiness. Inside and outside of the organization.

Money is a basic need but it doesn't fuel our need

for fulfillment and financial bonuses have been continuously proven to not increase work and life satisfaction.
Increasing these factors is the role of culture and contribution.

Rule #5: A Betterment culture is one that continually
incubates the qualities of humanity that future generations would be proud of.

Yes, your company is a culture incubator. It either incubates catabolic, destructive bacteria, such as that found
in rotting meat, or it incubates beneficial bacteria, such
as that found in Kombucha. The choice is yours!

Marketing

*Use of brand and personality to create consistent conversa-
tion that builds awareness and interest in a business.*

Rule #1: The purpose of marketing is to build awareness
of and interest in a product or service.

Focus on those two things when creating marketing cam-
paigns; awareness and interest.

Rule #2: Marketing, at its best, is about bettering the
world.

The best marketing authentically creates and shares
ways to create a better world through its products or services.

Rule #3: Marketing lays the foundation for building relationships.

Building interest and creating awareness are the foundation of creating profound customer relationships.

Rule #4: Marketing has value beyond the expenses it shows.

It is hard to see the full profitability of marketing without factoring in the intangibles that it creates in value for a company.

Rule #5: Marketing is always truthful and transparent.

If it isn't it doesn't fit the betterment model of marketing. There are countless examples, especially because of today's social media, of companyies who lost credibility and reputation due to their untruthful or inauthentic marketing practices. Companies, especially smaller ones who are beginning to be under more and more public scrutiny, can not afford to not be truthful or transparent.

Sales

The process of helping a person, group, or business entity to determine whether or not a company's products or services are of benefit to them.

Rule #1: The purpose of sales is NEVER to disorient, distract or deceive to make money. Ever.

Otherwise it isn't sales, it is tactical illusions being used for the purpose of stealing money.

<u>Rule #2</u>: "No" is not a reflection of you or your company.

If your company is operating with betterment sales and a prospective client says, "no" it could be for a few reasons. It could mean the value was not communicated effectively, which means changing or adapting sales processes Or, if it was communicated effectively, the product or service was not a good fit for them which is totally the customers choice. Either way leads to more understanding and betterment in your company regardless of the sale.

<u>Rule #3</u>: Sales should always be personal.

Selling is always a one-on-one feeling, even if it targets more than one person. It always speaks to someone on a personal level or else it isn't doing its job.

<u>Rule #4</u>: Sales requires bravery, but can easily turn into cunningness for those who aren't strong enough to accept failure or rejection.

Be brave. You are strong!

<u>Rule #5</u>: Nothing in business will have a chance to become better without sales.

Sales creates relationships that lead to customers which leads to revenue. Without sales, relationships are not effectively created on a scale that leads to profitability. You and your team need to be comfortable selling your products and services.

Customer Experience

All interactions a company has with those who have purchased their products and services.

<u>Rule #1</u>: Curiosity Eclipses Judgement.

All you need in customer service is curiosity. As soon as judgement occurs, you have already lost an opportunity to create a better relationship with a customer.

<u>Rule #2</u>: Build a Tribe.

The more ways that customers who love your products and services have to connect with you, the stronger and more loyal your customer base will get. This breeds sustainability through hard times as well as expansions.

<u>Rule #3</u>: Know what your customers want next (before they do).

Use the customer information you gather (that you have asked for) and the conversations you have to create trends and experiences that your customers didn't even know existed.

<u>Rule #4</u>: Loyal customers always become team members.

A team member, remember, is someone who supports the fulfillment of a product or service. Anyone externally who is doing this out of loyalty is also, by our definition, a team member.

Rule #5: There is no neutral customer.

Every single customer feels either positively or negatively about your company. A three star review is a non-committal 2 or 4 star review to avoid confrontation. Find out why.

One's Own

The mindset and tools used to navigate the different roles and hats worn inside and outside of work that impact an individual's health, happiness, wealth and fulfillment in life.

Purpose: What you feel you are here to experience.

Values: Both the omnipresent and consciously selected values that you hold in life.

Gifts: The things you naturally, or through practice, excel at.

Passions: The things you love to do or experience regardless of your skill level.

Contribution: What you do for work and for service to leave this world better than you came into it.

Connections: The intimate, family, social and professional relationships that impact you in your life.

<u>Physical Wellness</u>: What you do or want to do to become more physically healthy.

<u>Mental Wellness</u>: The mental activities you perform that keep your brain active and healthy.

<u>Emotional Wellness</u>: Your level of emotional intelligence, emotional connection and stress.

<u>Spiritual Wellness</u>: What you do to connect with whatever higher source (or natural source) you believe in.

<u>Abundance Indicator</u>: How much abundance you feel in life, on a scale from supremely abundant to completely full of scarcity.

<u>Enjoyment Indicator</u>: How much enjoyment you feel on a moment to moment basis.

16. THE BETTERMENT ASSESSMENT

The Betterment Assessment

I f you have gotten this far in the book and have been wondering, "Well, having the rules is nice, but how do I know how well my business compares to a true betterment business?" You aren't alone. For this reason, we have created the Betterment Assessment.

What Is It?

The betterment assessment is a free online assessment that you and other partners of your company can take to get a Betterment Rating and see where your company may not be performing optimally.

Why Should My Business Take It?

This assessment allows your company another tool or

indicator to see easy ways to move forward and get better. If you are an employee, or manager of the company, it allows you to have a communication tool for specific changes that can be made with some viable feedback to executives and other departments.

It also allows you to track team and department performance and give those members ways to perform better or ways to communicate with you changes that they feel can be made, especially to culture, leadership and management. This in turn allows you to become a better leader or manager.

Beyond that, it can allow you to become more aware of culture and make it more tangible within your leadership style.

For operations, it has been a godsend for companies who want their operative teams to think differently about operations and product and service development. It offers your operation team a perspective on all other aspects of business and customer experience that is affected by their operations actions.

Additionally, it can be used as a tool for active customers to judge your company based on their perception of it. What this means is you have legitimate feedback of how customers rate your businesses from a betterment perspective. Based on their answers, you will know where you need to grow or what you may not be conveying properly. For example, if one of the questions is, "Does company 'X' do anything for the community beyond providing services in exchange for money?" If a client answers, "No" or, "I don't know" but your company clearly holds a fundraiser every year, your company fundraiser marketing may not be reaching your target demographics.

For all of these reasons and more, the assessment can be a valuable, free asset to your company as a gift to you for the purchase of this book.

How Does It Work?

There is a mix of subjective and objective questions that will paint an entire picture of your business from all aspects of betterment that we discussed in part one and two of this book.

That link will take you to the assessment. Enter your name, company name and business email so we can send you the results and then the assessment will start!

When Will I Have The Results?

After the full assessment is completed and submitted, you will have an instant results page and a copy will be in your email to share with others or keep.

If you want to take the assessment, go here:

https://www.thenticate.biz/assessment

We hope this assessment is as helpful for your company as it has been for our multiple businesses and the countless others who use this assessment for betterment.

17. BETTERMENT IN ACTION

An Example of Business Betterment: Evolve Chocolate and Cafe

I n our research we looked at a number of businesses, small and large, to find one that we knew for certain exemplified the ideas and concepts within this book. We came across a local business in our hometown that literally fit the bill. We are excited to share our experience and their story with you!

Evolve Chocolate and Cafe, located in Bellingham, Washington is owned by wives, Shannon and Christy Fox. It is the culmination of a dream, hard work and strong values, led by trust and authenticity.

Evolve first started several years ago as a maker of fine and unique chocolate truffles and other delectables. With a website, a booth at the local farmer's market and pop-up stores around town they became a quick icon and symbol for success in the community. Not to mention they have great chocolates, and oh, also the incredible sipping chocolate topped with their homemade marshmallows!

In 2018, they moved into what they considered to be the perfect location on the top level of an iconic Bellingham bookstore in the historic Fairhaven district.

With their sense of community and connection to it, Shannon and Christy Fox saw this as an incredible opportunity to be a part of creating a deeper experience while sharing their love of food and nourishment.

As we talked with Shannon and Christy further about what excites them about being in business and what motivated them along with what they viewed as success, we were struck by the sincerity of their answers.

They described their love and respect for each other based on a foundation of trust. They also felt a passion for bringing this to their business.

Shannon describes the importance of trust in every relationship, including business relationships. In order to take risks in business, she says, you have to conduct yourself with authenticity and transparency (their words, not ours!). There has to be a trust with customers, your spouse, your partners, your vendors, and your staff. If you have that foundation, you'll get it right every time.

Operations

When it comes to running a business efficiently, the team

at Evolve Chocolate exemplifies the betterment mind-set.

As a business creating specialty chocolates, Evolve Chocolate effectively engaged with the community and key support systems in order to strengthen their brand and build sales while keeping quality standards high and overhead expenses low.

With a booth at the local and highly popular farmer's market, Evolve created a following based on their high quality, locally sourced ingredients and their commitment to building solid relationships with customers and the community.

They continued this effort of community connection through collaboration with local non-profit organizations by providing their products and services at charity events for little to no cost to the organization. This action not only enhanced their product awareness among attendees, but also garnered them a solid reputation as community supporters.

Efforts within this growing organization continued as they found additional ways to reach their customer base. One such way was to create pop up stores whereby they were not obligated to any long-term rental agreements and could react to market demand during peak seasons such as holiday seasons and throughout the year.

When identifying a space for their dream cafe, it was the landlord of the building that approached them initially. Because of their solid community relationships and customer following, they became a sought after business to take over space in an iconic and popular bookstore in town.

And, while the space had some limitations, this team used effective communication with resources to close the gap on those limitations, creating an environment that worked for their business and their customers.

They created an efficient and flexible operation with the space they had for creating and producing food products.

They have kept the vibe of former cafe locations, as a place for people to come and work, read, or relax while they enjoy their food and beverage by also adding additional seating surrounding the cafe and spilling out into the bookstore itself.

Knowing the kitchen space size was somewhat limiting, they have invoked an internal policy of zero waste and utilizing each ingredient in at least three different ways.

The cafe space is utilized as a community space as well for rent for business and special events.

Products And Services

Christy and Shannon feel that customer feedback is essential to providing a menu that is inclusive and what their customers are looking for when they are choosing to eat out or when they simply want something delectable and cozy with a good book to read.

They have an approach of diversifying their products. Some are available only for sale to eat at the cafe. Some are better when taken home to eat. Some are available in bulk. This approach allows them to be more adaptive to what is trending in food and in the community. This broad approach ensures that if one of their styles of offering is on a downtrend, the potential for another offering being on an uptrend keeps business and employees steadily working and engaging in essential business activities.

Leadership

Through a foundation of trust and a culture based on the culmination of experiences, Evolve Chocolate and Cafe clearly demonstrates our idea of leadership at every level. Staff are visibly encouraged to engage with Christy and Shannon as well as make decisions in their absence that benefit the experience of customers.

There are many styles of leadership that one can adopt. Through observation, it truly appears that the two owners use adaptive and transformational leadership, depending on the moment and situation, to encourage as often as possible for their employees to be their own leaders. They challenge everyone to take initiative, ownership and a critical approach to their work.

Management

When it comes to managing their team, owners Shannon and Christy definitely take an inclusive approach. They ask the question, "how are we able to create a work/life balance for ourselves if we don't create a team that allows us to do just that?" Their approach to managing their team is based on empowerment through communication and learning. Each staff person is involved in the why's of the business as well as the decision making that may be necessary if Shannon or Christy are not onsite at times.

This allows the owners to create workers who can become self-sufficient. The people who stick around are passionate about learning, about food and about quality. Christy and Shannon nurture and feed these passions. In turn, this makes management more often than not a delight and seamless experience that allows them to focus on other important business workings.

Team

When you walk into Evolve Chocolate and Cafe, and when you get to know Shannon and Christy, the way they utilize their "team" is not only obvious, but inspiring.

As they talk about their team, Christy and Shannon use words such as trust, support, and collaboration. With this foundation of trust, they have succeeded in creating an environment of mutual success among everyone individually as well as for the business.

Their low turnover in an industry with considerably high turnover, especially in a college town, goes to show how integral and rewarding the experience of Evolve is. Not only to the customer, but to the employee.

Culture

The vibe and overall feeling from Evolve Chocolate and Cafe is one of positivity, comfort, and inclusiveness. And, as a business that creates a business betterment path, this overall feeling is set by the owners, staff, and customers based on each unique experience with the business. The staff clearly enjoys being there as is seen in their interaction with customers and Christy and Shannon.

Because the kitchen and working areas are rather compact, it almost feels as if the customer is a part of the experience and along for the ride just as much as the employees. In a way, when employees go from on-duty to off-duty, they become customers.

Christy and Shannon truly have created an experience where they are rooted and integrated into Fairhaven, into the bookstore, and into the community.

Marketing

Marketing efforts by Evolve Chocolate and Cafe truly calls into play the importance of creating a message that mirrors the values and mission of the business. Their mission is delivering high-quality tasty food utilizing as many local sources as possible. They also follow up this mission by creating a space that is comfortable for guests and a reflection of their own personalities.

Everything they say and do reflects this mission. Everything they say in their market communicates this mission.

By asking for continuous feedback from their team members and their customers, Evolve Chocolate and Cafe is actively making tweaks and updates to their products and services. They understand that they aren't the only two that know people in the community, and they are always looking for new vendor relationships and quality ingredients. They communicate this in their marketing to customers, involving them in the hunt and conversation about quality.

Their logo and marketing materials succinctly reflect their mission, their passion, and their own personalities.

Sales

Sales for Evolve Chocolate and Cafe are really driven by reputation, quality of experience, relationships and word of mouth.

They have taken it to a different level by offering some of those ingredients they use in their own menu, such as honey and coffee, for sale at a kiosk by their front ordering counter.

They also prepare, as an added incentive for sales, their artisan chocolates and other goodies perched on the counter ready to take home.

Their day-long menu reflects items that cater to different diets and tastes. They adapt this often, more often than most businesses we have seen, with requests, seasonal availability of fresh ingredients, and local favorites.

Customer Experience

There are a lot of unique and wonderful feelings in the world. Going to a bookstore with a fireplace and sitting to relax is a positive memory many of us may have. Evolve heightens that memory and sense of comfort to an extraordinary level.

Picture this scene, one that happens on a daily basis;

A local or city visitor walks into the bookstore. They take their time perusing the three-stories of towering shelves and find a perfect new book to read. While waiting to checkout, they smell a mix of sweet and savory aromas waft through. Upon checkout, they are told about a cafe and chocolate lounge upstairs. They go upstairs to see what they have.

At the top of the stairs, they see it; a cafe lined in plants and herbs, framing a display of goods with steam and bustling cooks preparing food in the background. They walk closer to take a peek at the menu. They are surprised to see a menu filled with local meats and vegetables, appetizers, soups, salads and entrees that look, smell, and sound like they would be served at a 5-star restaurant.

The current teller asks if she can answer any questions for them, or if they would like to look at the specials. After a pleasant conversation and some thorough information, they choose to get a polenta bowl with roasted beets, squash crema, goat cheese, and an apple-chili gastrique. They decide to add a taste of the 85% sipping chocolate, because, why not!

After ordering, they sit down over the expansive, bright-but-cloud-covered view of Ferndale and Bellingham Bay. Shannon personally brings them their food, telling them to just knock on the open kitchen door frame if they need anything else. They enjoy the rest of their time eating a wonderful meal and digging into their new book.

This experience is not uncommon. In fact, it is the norm and the standard. And it is just a glimpse of the effect of the hard work that Shannon and Christy have crafted to ensure their customer experience is beyond stellar, every time.

One's Own

Life balance is extremely important to Shannon and Christy. As a married couple working together, they have worked hard to find the right team around them to support their efforts for time off, time together and their own personal self-care. Through solid trust, Christy now leaves each Tuesday at noon to take the time she needs to reinvigorate and regenerate.

Life and relationships can be difficult and challenging *without* the added stress of running a business together. So a dedication to this balance is truly a key plan and strategy for its success as a whole.

They not only have to consider the mental, physical, and emotional well being for themselves, but also for each other. They also choose to take these into consideration for their employees as well.

Knowing how important these things are for longevity and business sustainability, they recognize that this is the case for their workers and ensure they are keeping tabs on how they are doing, so they can figure out how to support their employees if something is off.

To Christy and Shannon, this consideration for their employees means an equal trust, commitment from them and keeps them fully productive. It also shows their workers that they truly and genuinely care about their wellbeing.

Overall, no business is perfect, but with how fast Evolve has become a staple in the community and considering the level of standard they did it with, Evolve is a wonderful example of a betterment business.

There will always be ways to improve. There will always be ways to do better. There will always be room for growth. But a solid foundation of betterment will ensure that those journeys forward are always done the right way. And even if the right way isn't the easy way, it will always produce an unwavering sense of reward and accomplishment without compromise to integrity or reputation.

WHAT'S NEXT?

This ending is not the end

You've made it to the end of the F*ck Growth! Congratulations. You now have a better understanding of the movement, conscious capitalism and a method of business that is sustainable from a profit and global business health. So where do we go from here?

Create a Conversation

The first and easiest thing to do is to start a conversation. In your office, at business lunches, on social media, with family and friends that are interested and anywhere that you think this information is viable. Change starts one person at a time. The more people that can shift their perception of growth, the more we can turn the tables and ultimately change an entire business culture and mindset as we know it.

Betterment Assessment

If you haven't yet, go to our website and take the free assessment. See how your business stacks up to the betterment model. There is no reason not to! www.Thenticate.biz

Take Action

While you're at our website, you might as well check out our blog. We continually publish information related to betterment in every area of business that is relevant or timeless. We also keep up to date information on financial and economic markets and how to navigate them for betterment and sustainability.

Connect with Us on Social Media

We love engaging with business owners who have questions or comments. You can reach us on all of our platforms!

Facebook.com/Thenticate
Twitter.com/Thenticate
Instagram.com/Thenticate

On all of our social media platforms we try to answer every question and comment. We post updates on our events, webinars and other free offerings. And we just in general love connecting with you all!

F*CK Growth Guides

(Coming soon!) As of 2020 we are already in the works for workbooks and checklists on each of the betterment areas of business and life. Keep a lookout for these guide books that will give your company a step by step approach for combing through and creating betterment.

FREQUENTLY ASKED QUESTIONS

...And other information

Over the years, we have received quite a few questions. Here are the most common questions that we receive that are relevant to F*CK Growth.

Where did the betterment mindset come from?

The betterment mindset came from us! Jesse and Jennifer. It is a culmination of our experiences, perspectives, education and observations of multiple industries and sizes of businesses. You could also say that it came from multiple conversations and cups of coffee. Multiple years of different issues and band-aid solutions that, to us, just didn't fill the current void that is in business that no one talks about because it's not an urgent or priority conversation when money isn't tight. You could also say it comes from a place of a need for something more sustainable that our current generations, entrepreneurs and business owners are searching for on a deeper level.

How long has this been going on?

Since 2017. That is when this concept hit its infancy and we have been tinkering with it ever since. We think these universal concepts are beyond us and have been expressed individually in many different ways of many eras in business. We just feel they have never been expressed quite this way.

Who is Thenticate?

Thenticate is a fusion of Jennifer and Jesse's values, experience and missions in business. Thenticate focuses on coaching and education for business owners of all shapes and sizes. When consulting, Jennifer and Jesse meet the client where they are, uncover exactly why businesses aren't where they want to be and make a plan on how to get there through any obstacles.

More recently, Thenticate has become an online resource for articles, videos and more that looks to merge business and personal balance struggles to help business owners, entrepreneurs and executives experience more of what they want out of life and less of what they don't.

What other books does Thenticate have?

F*CK GROWTH is the first of its kind! Jennifer and Jesse are focusing on writing and planning workbooks for each area of business that we have touched on in this book. These workbooks will be step-by-step guides for implementing all of the betterment mindset rules that we have outlined here.

What services does Thenticate provide?

Below are Thenticates services, which are all offered virtually or in person.

Online business betterment assessment (free)

We offer a free assessment that seeks to answer one question: how does your business stack up to our betterment model? It is thorough and should offer a realistic way for you and your team to move forward. Feel free to take the assessment on our website!

Half-day business discovery session

We call it the Think Tank. We take a half-day with you and whoever you want to participate in your team to uncover any blocks and opportunities in every aspect of your business.

After the session, we build a report that you and your team can use to take action, or work with us to build a more extensive plan.

Coaching sessions with Jennifer, Jesse or both

If you have completed the Think Tank session with us, and would like to continue working with us, we offer a flexible variety of ways to support you in your business journey to betterment.

Books and physical training materials

F*CK Growth is far from our last offering of business education on the betterment mindset. We look to offer more books and resources over 2020 and beyond.

Business Betterment Workshops

Throughout this year and beyond, we will also be offering digital and in person workshops for businesses to make impactful steps forward in a short period of time in terms of betterment planning and strategy for your business.

Public speaking events by request

If your business would like us to come speak to your team or for a business event, please visit our website to inquiry. We would love to be a part of your business betterment.

If you have a question that wasn't answered here...

www.thenticate.biz

has even more resources and forums where we answer questions that get asked and updated continuously. Additionally, our Facebook Group (search for "Thenticate's Vibrant Business Group") is where we often connect for more personal and detailed questions than on our social medias.

ABOUT THE AUTHORS

Jennifer Dodge

Jennifer holds vast experience in the corporate and real-estate fields. She is a self-taught content strategist and content marketer who has been helping businesses hone in on the essence of their business and communicate that effectively to their customers for almost ten years. Her ultimate goal is to help businesses and people find their center.

Jennifer is an animal lover and avid cook who spends as much of her time as possible with her two daughters and family as she can.

Jesse Nunley

Jesse is an enthusiast of the business of health from both a consumer and practitioner perspective. He comes from a long line of entrepreneurs. He has a degree in business, human resources, and is a certified business and health coach. He currently owns and operates multiple businesses, including a chiropractic and massage practice in Bellingham, Washington. His ultimate goal is to be an angel investor for businesses he believes in across the world. To do speaking, mentoring and writing full time.

Jesse, his wife and young children love traveling, being outdoors and enjoying the wide variety of activities the Pacific Northwest has to offer.

ABOUT THENTICATE

We (Jesse Nunley and Jennifer Dodge) began as two local entrepreneurs seeking ways to grow our respective businesses in innovative ways while also looking for synergies in like-minded people that could add support to our own respective goals.

We met about three years ago in a local networking group in Bellingham, Washington. Knowing there was a certain synergy between our two businesses of content marketing and business coaching we set out to uncover our collective purpose and how we might build on the obvious common search for purpose we both had and still have today.

When we initially formed Thenticate, we knew we wanted to help businesses and people be the best they can be while creating strategies for business growth utilizing our own experiences and expertise. Our own journey started with the idea of a written "manifesto," of all of our ideas, thoughts and suggestions on how to grow business, while simultaneously being thoughtful about how to grow business. We included all of the traditional concepts of marketing and human resources and operations but really worked to take it to the next level of looking within the true inner workings of a business.

Business was definitely off to a slow start as we tried to be louder than all of the noise doing the same thing: telling people how to create a stronger business. We knew we were different in our transparent and deeper thoughtfulness when it came to creating a sustainable business. What we didn't consider at the time was that, while our thinking may be different, our approach was not the unique approach we intended when it came to working with different businesses individually. The operative word being individually. What we had come to realize is that businesses need individual attention and that attention must be very customized based on a whole slew of things that make up that particular businesses ecosystem.

What we ultimately discovered is that we were trying to put a square peg into a round hole. One size does not fit all when it comes to how to manage, create and run a business in a very thoughtful way.

We set out to fully discover what creates a stronger business. And, what we found after countless hours with business owners and their teams was that those businesses who saw themselves and their businesses as a solid authentic reflection of themselves were the strongest. This reflected in the implementation of their business mission. Their goals were always on their way to creating a better business that showed sustainable growth as a side effect.

We worked with businesses who weren't afraid to stop, and go back to what was important to them. Businesses who created connections with their teams and resources, and who exhibited transparency and honesty with their customers. Who were committed to giving back to their community by executing decisions based on those values which originally drove them to create or become involved and these businesses actually saw growth and additional success as a result.

We started to call this amazing process 'business betterment.' What it means to us is going back to what is truly important to individuals and the community and creating strategies and tactics to move forward based on those intrinsic and very personal values. It is the "why" of why we got into business to begin with. And it is so much more as well. When you go back to that idea of sustainability-based growth, because you just cannot continue doing business as usual, you realize what is important to you and your business. Combining this broader thought process to your current daily activities including those numbers in the spreadsheet, opens the doors to a better understanding of your business health and paves the way for sustainable success.

A FAREWELL

A message for our readers

We wanted to say goodbye before you continue on your business and life journey. A personal note to you of sorts.

If you are reading this. Thank you. For seeing this book. For wanting to have a better business. For wanting to serve more people. We wish we knew you more personally, because those things alone make you someone we could partner with to build a better world.

We have put a lot of thought and consideration into this process so it can be something that lives beyond us. You are how it lives beyond this, no matter when you are reading this. This world will always need entrepreneurs to stand up and find creative solutions for caring for our planet, for people and for empowering others. Even more than that, it needs entrepreneurs who are willing to do so without compromise. Who has a will so strong that despite being told "that can't be done" or "that's impossible", they unwaveringly create a reality that the world can't help but acknowledge and take as Truth.

Everything was impossible before someone did it. This is the road of pioneers. If you are one such person, know that it will not be easy. You will be tested. You will be challenged. There will always be an enticing shortcut, way to cheat or expend less time, energy and income to gain an advantage. This is how good intentions and good ideas become destructive companies.

Stay strong, know who you are, know your vision and let your aim be true.

Sincerely,

Jesse and Jennifer

www.ingramcontent.com/pod-product-compliance
Lightning Source LLC
LaVergne TN
LVHW052021080426
835513LV00018B/2103